To the memory of Lawrence Graburn

Dedicated to:-
his grandsons, Andrew and Michael,
and great grandchildren, Jamie and Sarah.

First Published in 2001 by
Southern Heritage Books,
35 Salvington Hill,
Worthing,
West Sussex. BN13 3BB

Text ©: Lawrence Graburn and Christopher A Hare

ISBN 0-9527097-3-2

Printed by RPM, 2-3 Spur Road, Quarry Lane, Chichester, West Sussex. PO19 2PR.

Good Old, Bad Old Days

- the Sussex of Lawrence Graburn

Edited by Chris Hare

Chris Hare

Acknowledgements

The author and the family of Lawrence Graburn would like to thank the *West Sussex Gazette* for permission to reprint articles first published in that newspaper; the Peake family for permission to re-print the sketches drawn by Mervyn Peake; the West Sussex Library Service for permission to reproduce photographs and drawings in their possession (which are also individually acknowledged). The author would like to thank Kim Leslie at West Sussex Records Office for suggesting the idea of this book, and for putting him in touch with Rosamund Hoy, Lawrence Graburn's daughter. The author and the family of Lawrence Graburn would like to thank West Sussex County Council for the generous donation they made towards the publication costs of this book. Thanks are also due to John Goulding of Optimus Books, Worthing, who proof-read the text and produced the index. The original paintings reproduced in colour in this book were presented to the Graburn family by the artists, and still remain in the possession of the family.

Contents

INTRODUCTION

I first came across the writings of Lawrence Graburn in 1986. I was working for Arun District Council at that time, and my job then included devising a series of "heritage trails" across the district, to include as many areas of historical interest as possible. It was while searching through the newspaper cuttings files, kept in the reference section at Worthing Library, that I came across a series of fascinating articles, penned by someone calling himself "Newall Duke". The articles, published in the *West Sussex Gazette* during the 1950's and early 1960's, were quite unlike any others that I had read. They were noteworthy for the diversity of local topics covered, from local history to natural history, from folklore to tales of the old hunting days in Sussex. Yet, more than that, they attracted my attention because the writer of the articles, far from being a researcher like myself, uncovering the past from written sources, was, more often than not, speaking from personal experience. On other occasions he would quote from the memories of old people he had known and spoken to in earlier days. Yet his identity and place of residence remained a mystery.

It was through Kim Leslie at the West Sussex Records Office that I was put in contact with Mrs. Rosamund Hoy, the daughter of Lawrence Graburn. It transpired that for many years she had been keen to see the articles of her late father published in book form, and so it was that I learned the true identity of "Newall Duke".

Lawrence Newall Graburn was born at Wepham in the parish of Burpham in 1881. His father, Mr. Newall Graburn, was the tenant of the Duke of Norfolk at Wepham Farm, and had inherited the farm from his father, Thomas Graburn, who had moved to Sussex from Lincolnshire in 1861. Newall Graburn had married a member of the Duke family, who had farmed in West Sussex for centuries: it was once possible to ride from Chichester to Steyning without leaving land farmed by a member of this family. When Lawrence Graburn came to write his articles, he acknowledged this ancient downland clan, as well as his father's family, by writing under the pseudonym "Newall Duke" ("Newall" was a Christian name used for many generations by the Graburns).

Graburn turned to writing following the depression in agriculture that descended upon many Sussex farms in the 1930's. It was no longer possible to make the farm at Wepham pay, so Graburn was forced to give up his tenancy. Had he waited a few months longer, the outbreak of the Second World War might have reversed his fortunes and made the farm profitable again. Yet it was precisely because he found himself, at 58, with no obvious purpose in life, that his friends persuaded him to write down some of the tales of old Sussex with which he had become so familiar. He had a particular affinity with the country people and their ways. As his daughter Rosamund remembers: "He loved the village, he loved the countrymen, all the old characters - the old villagers - and they loved him." One of his grandsons, Michael Hoy, remembers being taken around the village by his grandfather, and being told the story of every house and cottage and their occupants.

During the war years, Graburn spent many long hours in the cottages of the old country people, some of whose memories stretched back to the 1860's and 70's, back indeed to the time when his family first arrived in the village. Many more examples of country lore and history were noted down by Graburn at livestock fairs and in the tap-rooms of village pubs, and in particular in the George and Dragon at Burpham.

On 1 December 1940, Graburn began to write down his recollections and observances in a hard-covered exercise book. This book became both a journal of current events, largely associated with the life of the immediate country district, and a repository for the rich oral history that he recorded from the retired rural labourers of the district, as well as from his own experiences, and those of his father and grandfather before him. It is a unique document, which he kept writing until his death at the age of 83 in 1965.

The first page of the journal gives a clear indication of Graburn's loves and interests. Two short verses are preceded by a simple introduction, which reads: "Notes on Burpham and people and Natural History written by L.N.Graburn in the hope that they may someday interest somebody." One of the verses, written by Lindsay-Gordon states:

> If once we efface the joys of the chase
> From the land and outroot the stud,
> Goodbye to the Anglo-Saxon race,
> Farewell to the Norman blood.

The other verse, very sentimental, declares:

> There are men both good and wise who hold that in a future state
> Dumb creatures we have cherished here below
> Shall give us greeting when we pass the golden gate.

To many people today the love of animals and nature in general appears strangely at odds with an equal love of hunting and "the chase", yet to country people in the recent past, and to some even now, there was no contradiction. Hunting defined and gave focus to a rural way of life: it answered a practical purpose, it brought the community together, while reinforcing the social hierarchy, and it created drama and excitement in a world that was both mundane and predictable by modern standards. While reading the articles contained within this book, it is good to remember that although they were written less than fifty years ago, they recall people, places and events that are so very different from our own times, and grounded in values we have largely abandoned.

Rosamund recalls that her father never went out without three items in his pocket: some string, a shilling and a penknife. The string was there to mend anything from a broken stirrup to a bootlace; the penknife was to cut the same, or to kill or skin an animal, such as a rabbit caught in a snare; and the shilling was to pay a country person, who helped you with your horse, or opened a gate to allow a quick entrance (particularly during a hunt). Curious, anachronistic and outdated they may be, but these items and their uses reflect the reality of life in the villages of the South Downs before the Second World War.

I am currently researching a book for the West Sussex Records Office, which will look at aspects of social change in the county since the late nineteenth century. Part of this research has involved interviewing Sussex-born people about their perceptions of change during that time. Many of those living in the Arundel/ Burpham area mentioned Lawrie Graburn during their interviews. All the memories were good ones. Jack O'Neil remembered his informality, and how, "he liked the ordinary working people - he didn't care for dressing up." Margery Cobby remembers that he "was such a kind person," who used to talk to her mother about the old days. Jean Forster recalled that her father, the village blacksmith, was a great friend of Graburn's, and that the two would talk for hours about matters of common interest. After Graburn's death, he used to write letters to the *West Sussex Gazette* on matters of local interest - "I think there was a little bit of Lawrie Graburn rubbing off on him," Jean explained. Frank Penfold, a founder of the Sussex Wildlife Trust, remembered his long conversations with him about natural history, and that he had "a great interest in anything local." That Graburn and his work should still be so vividly recalled thirty-six years after his death is a testimony to the high regard in which he was held by the people who lived, and still do live in that part of Sussex.

It was soon after the War that Graburn began writing articles with a view to having them published. Some of his earliest articles appeared in the *Sussex County Magazine*, others followed in *The Field*, and in various farming and hunting magazines. However it was the *West Sussex Gazette* that proved his mainstay, and it was in the *West Sussex Gazette* that he wrote as Newall Duke. Articles appeared regularly, and at least once a month between 1953 and his death twelve years later. It is only possible to re-print a selection in this book, but hopefully it is a representative one. Where appropriate, I have added further information to the original articles, including the letters that readers wrote in response to the memories that Graburn had stirred. During the early twentieth century, a number of literary and artistic figures were resident in Burpham. In particular John Cowper Powys and Tickner Edwardes, both of whom Graburn knew, wrote extensively about the locality and its people, and I have quoted from their works where they shed further light on the topics covered by Graburn in his articles. The colour plates that appear in this book are reproduced from originals painted by artists resident in the village.

In this book you will find an extraordinary diversity of topics covered. In an effort to impose some order on the material, I have grouped the articles into two sections. The first deals with People, with local history, folklore and farming; while the second deals with natural history and the "nature notes" that appear in the journal. It would probably have been possible to create further categories, yet even with two there are obvious overlaps. Unlike the narrowly-focused academic, Lawrie Graburn had an all encompassing interest in the world around him and was not limited by "terms of reference" or "schools of thought" or anything that might have impeded his curiosity and desire to know more about the country and people with whom he grew up.

In these pages you will find accounts that are factual, others that are humorous. Sometimes you will be left pining for a more innocent and simple "lost world", while at others you may be thankful that you are not living in such ignorant or unjust times. The allure of the days before motor cars, aeroplanes and a myriad of other mechanical sounds obliterated the sounds of nature has to be set against the consideration that poverty and low wages were the norm and education was a luxury for the few. Apart from such vivid contrasts, this book also offers the unexpected: tales of village justice and "rough music", of feuds that lasted for years and fights between villages that saw the shedding of much blood; there are stories of ghosts and the supernatural and of the spot where Jack Upperton the highwayman was gibbeted; all combined with acutely observed features on local wildlife and tall tales of hunts and huntsmen.

Finally, it is perhaps worth making the point that these "bad old, good old days" did not vanish all that long ago. One of the articles that follows concerns "the runners" or itinerant workers, often of gypsy origin, who were once a common sight in the country of the South Downs. These folk lived rough and ready lives, rarely having either "proper" homes or jobs. They survived through seasonal work, scavenging and poaching.

Both Rosamund and Michael Hoy remember an old couple, who were still living in the village until about 1973. Their cottage had one electric light, one tap and one small kitchen sink. They sat on piles of newspapers and slept on the same. They took no baths because they had no bath. They had no toilet facilities, but deposited their sewage from buckets into pits in their garden, which in turn provide manure for their vegetable patch. These vegetables they sold to others in the village, including the Graburns. As Rosamund recalls, her mother always used to caution the maid to "make sure you wash them well."

Michael remembers, when he was a boy, how the old chap used to take, "Gem", the Graburn family dog, for "walks". One day Michael accompanied "Old Charlie" on one of these expeditions through the woods and found out just why he was so keen for the dog to accompany him:

"...We were going up Green's Lane, when Gem suddenly pounced into the bushes and he managed to get hold of a pheasant, which he quickly killed by breaking its neck. He came out of the bushes, and I was saying, 'look Gem's got a pheasant! Gem's got a pheasant!', and Charlie was saying, 'Don't tell everyone about it - keep quiet!' Then he grabbed the pheasant by its legs and then something happened that I've never quite seen in my life before - he seemed to have a cavernous pocket that was sown into his trousers and he unhitched some kind of clip or something at the top and a full section opened up - and he simply put this pheasant into this pocket and closed it up again, and it was like you wouldn't even believe it was there...and all this happened in a matter of seconds...and very quickly the pheasant disappeared and that was it - we just carried on walking as if nothing had happened."

Such stories of poaching exploits, some even more bizarre than this one, appear in Graburn's articles. Yet whereas these events date back to the late nineteenth and early twentieth century, Old Charlie was still at it in the 1970's. But, as Michael says, he represented the "tail-end of an era".

"Popular" histories sometimes seem to play on our latent sense of nostalgia, appealing to our belief that somehow the past was better than the present. Rosamund herself remembers the days when she was a child, waking up not to the sound of motor cars, but to the "clip-clop of the cart horses going to and fro". Yet she also remembers the harsh side of life, particularly for the farm workers:

"I always felt sorry for the old farm workers because they never had any adequate clothing. They had to go and work even if it was pouring with rain - I saw them coming home with sacks round their shoulders. I mean a sack is no good - they never had a waterproof, there was no plastic then, no plastic feed sacks they could use...they got soaked to the skin...it was awful. It was a very hard life they had."

This is a view more familiar in the pages of academic histories, where the writer is keen to highlight class conflicts and underline the political implications of human endeavour. One of the great merits of the articles that follow is that they give both sides of the picture: the pleasure and the pain. Such insights were available to Graburn because they came from the people who had directly experienced them. What follows is a direct link with the Sussex of one hundred and one hundred and fifty years ago - warts and all.

Chris Hare, Worthing, November 2001

Lawrence Graburn standing by the Gibbet memorial he erected
with G. Hayler at Blakehurst in 1951.

Lawrence Graburn on his horse by "The Splash" in 1913.

Lawrie Graburn on horse, outside Wepham House, c. 1905.

Wepham House, home to the Graburn from 1861 until the early 1930s.
This photograph dates from c. 1880, before renovation.

"Old Ratty" drawn by Mervyn Peake.

"Old Mark" drawn by Mervyn Peake.

The Squire and the Mushroom-picker, drawn by Mervyn Peake.

Farmer Duke's quart-sized glass, especially made so the gout-ridden farmer could obey his doctor's order only to drink one glass of Port per day!

Sir Harry Johnston, Agnes Graburn's uncle, was a colonial administrator, who retired to Poling, and died there in 1927. He wrote about the Sussex countryside in his autobiography.

Reproduced courtesy of West Sussex Library Service.

John Cowper Powys, the famous writer lived in Burpham in the early twentieth century. He wrote about the village in his 1934 autobiography.

Reproduced courtesy of West Sussex Library Service.

Rev. Tickner Edwardes, Vicar of Burpham 1927–1935, but resident
since c. 1897. Edwardes was an astute observer of country ways.
Reproduced courtesy of West Sussex Library Service.

W. H. Hudson, the writer and naturalist, wrote extensively about the Sussex
countryside in his book, *Nature in Downland*, first published in 1900.
Reproduced courtesy of West Sussex Library Service.

ROUGH MUSIC
An effective village punishment

Hearing a discussion recently in the village inn on "rough music", and never having witnessed it myself, I went to see an old man in our village who had taken part in one of these occasions 60 years ago. He told me that this was the last one performed in the village, although other places had them for several years longer. His father, who had lived all his life here, and had taken part many times in these demonstrations, had told him that they always did good and a second visit was seldom necessary.

He went on to say that a man who ill-treated his wife or children would be warned to mend his ways. If this had no effect, a time (at night) and a place outside the village would be arranged for the band to meet. To this spot all the men and boys of the village would go, armed with anything that made a noise - horns, drums, old tin cans, and whistles. They then started off; their leader wearing a battered top hat and carrying a stick, which he used to beat time to the music.

As they went through the village, the noise they made was deafening and roused the people from their beds. Windows opened as people peered out to watch the crowd go by. They all knew that the music was for Jack Smith, who had been knocking his missus about on his return from the pub on Saturday nights. Approaching a cart-horse stable adjoining the road, the leader put up his hand saying, "'Old 'ard, we don't want all they 'osses to break loose in there." In the sudden silence that followed all that could be heard was the tramp and clatter of hobnail boots on the flint road until the stables had been passed.

On reaching the house of the culprit, the noise increased in violence until the leader called a halt. They then chanted some lines, of which my informant could only remember the last two:

> He beat her black, he beat her blue,
> He made her rattle through and through.

If there was no improvement after this in the man's behaviour to his wife or children, a second visit would be made. This time his effigy would be carried at the head of the procession and burnt outside his house, to the noise of yells and bangs. Dire threats were shouted by the assembled mob, while dancing round the burning effigy, which looked rather like a Guy Fawkes dummy.

"Rough Music" varied a great deal in different parts of the country, and is known to have been carried on for hundreds of years. It gave great pleasure to the youth of the village, when there were not so many distractions as there are today. No-one in authority ever seemed to object, but apparently gave it their blessing.

First published in the *West Sussex Gazette*, 27 May 1954

Rough Music expressed the indignation of the community for an "offence" which in some way outraged the collective morality of the village. Men who beat their wives or parents who cruelly ill-used their children were the most common targets. Usually both the victims and the perpetrators of rough music came from the ranks of the common people, but occasionally these demonstrations could be directed against their social superiors. In my book, Historic Worthing - the Untold Story, I give two instances, from the mid-nineteenth century, of upper middle-class victims of the mob.

Both were newcomers to the town, one a lady, the other a gentleman, and both had given offence by their conduct towards local women. As Lawrie Graburn noted in his article, rough music could well receive the "blessing" of those in authority, and that was probably the case in these two examples, where a proportion at least of "respectable" opinion overlooked or even connived in the rough music displays.

Graburn also mentioned the similarity between the effigy-burning that took place as part of a rough music demonstration, and that witnessed on Bonfire Night. The analogy was well made, for often November 5th was the occasion for the biggest and most violent displays of victimisation. Such riotous conduct was a common feature of life in Victorian Sussex. However towards the end of he nineteenth century, respectable opinion began to turn against mob-rule, whatever its supposed justifications. An increase in the manpower of the West Sussex Constabulary, and the growing determination of magistrates to use their powers to quell tumultuous street demonstrations, explains in part, the decline of rough music from the 1870's onwards.

Not surprisingly, rough music disappeared in the towns first, where police numbers were higher, and persisted in the more remote rural districts, where tradition was more ingrained and police numbers far fewer. In October 1873, a policeman from Littlehampton intervened to stop a display of rough music at Wick. The result was a violent confrontation between the constable and the rough music-makers, which led to three Lyminster men being brought before the magistrates on a charge of assault. The following account, which appeared in the West Sussex Gazette *at the time, is interesting, not just for its description of the rough music, but also for what it tells us about youthful attitudes towards the police at the time:*

Three young men of Lyminster were charged with assaulting P.C. Reed, on the 20th October last - Mr. George Lear appeared for the defence. From the evidence of the constable it appeared that on the evening of the 20th, at about a quarter past seven, he was called to a disturbance that was taking place at Wick.

On reaching the Globe Inn he found thirty or forty boys outside making a great noise with tin kettles and other instruments, in fact, treating some unfortunate person to "rough music". There was also a great noise inside the house, and after he had waited outside some little time the three defendants and others came out. Two of the defendants, Mills and Williams, had their faces blackened, and directly they got outside they commenced beating their "instruments" up the street. They would not desist from their noise, although requested several times to do so by the constable.

When near the Dewdrop Inn the constable attempted to take away Morley's "instrument", an old tin dish, when he dropped it and struck the constable twice in the face with his fist. The other defendants then came up and collared the constable and held him against the wall. When they released him they again resumed their "music" down the street, and he then attempted to take away Mills' "instrument", a tea tray, when the other two held him against the wall, and pushed him about in a very rough manner.

The constable then went to Littlehampton, and in company with the sergeant returned to the Globe Inn, where they saw Morley and Williams who refused to give their names. Mills, whom they discovered at the Dewdrop, also refused. He was quite certain as to the identity of the defendants - the constable was cross-examined by Mr. Lear as to the identity of the prisoners, but he said he was perfectly sure that Morley hit him. An elderly man, named Stephen Hammond, was called for the defence, and he swore that Morley had his face blackened (the constable stated that he had not), and that it was a man, who went by the name of "Sergeant", who struck the constable in the face with a stick whilst the officer was endeavouring to wrench a tray away from him. "Sergeant" bolted the next day. He never saw either of the defendants strike the constable.[5]

The magistrates, in a diplomatic decision which probably pleased neither side, found all three men guilty of assaulting the constable by pushing him around, but not of the more serious charge of having punched him in the face. They were fined 10s 8d each, including costs, the best part of a week's wage for young labouring men in those days. In default of payment they were to be imprisoned with hard labour for fourteen days. However, as often happened in such instances, "the money was easily found", by which were can assume the men's family and friends contributed to raising the sum required.

Following Graburn's original article, several older readers wrote in to the Gazette with their memories of rough music: back in 1954, a person aged seventy or over could well have remembered such events. Lillian Brown, then living in Cuckfield, remembered the days of her youth, when she lived at Bury. In that village the rough-musickers referred to themselves as the "Kangaroo Band" (any connection there with "kangaroo court", I wonder?), and Mrs. Brown well recalled the verses they used to holler out on such occasions:

> There is a man lives in this place
> He beat his wife - a sad disgrace!
> He beat her black, he beat her blue;
> He made her poor bones rattle, too.
>
> Now if this man don't mend his manners
> We'll have to send him to the tanner's;
> And if the tanner don't tan him well
> We'll nail him on a nail in hell
>
> And if that nail should chance to crack
> He'll fall upon the Devil's back;
> And should the Devil chance to run
> We'll shoot him with this fiery gun.[4]

At the end of the last stanza a gun would be fired, presumably in the air, rather than at the miscreant or his property. J. S. Chandler recalled his boyhood in a Hampshire village, where rough music was a fairly common occurrence. He remembered that the victims were usually middle-aged, childless couples, and rarely younger couples with children. Also men rather than women were the general targets; seldom did a wife receive the same punishment for similar conduct. Chandler recounted one rough music demonstration that rather backfired on the demonstrators:

"My father told me of a rough musicking against a butcher in the village, who was supposed to have ill-treated his wife. When the demonstration was at its height, the butcher filled his blunderbuss with blood and fired it at the crowd. The blood was well spread and the crowd quickly dispersed, thinking that some of their number had been shot."[5]

Chandler added that rough music "no doubt left its mark and was a warning to others. Being bound over or being sent to prison would not have had the lasting effect that rough musicking had in the days of my youth." He thought that the custom died out in his village during the 1880's.

Another correspondent, signing himself "An Arundelian", thought that rough music continued for about another twenty years in Arundel. He had witnessed such a demonstration in the Ford Road, where "a party of young men" were "lustily banging tins and old buckets at the object of their dislike." He also recalled one of the "serenaders" telling him that they were within the law "while they kept on the move", but if they remained outside the house they were "causing a riot", and liable to prosecution.[6] In those days the Riot Act was still in force (it was not repealed until 1966), although, as already stated, it was rare for the authorities to intervene in a

15

rough music demonstration until after 1870.

The last display of rough music in West Sussex may have been at Clapham, just before the First World War. On that occasion an element of farce entered the proceedings when it was realised that one of the men with a blackened face, shouting at the top of his voice was none other than the target of the demonstration! Like so many rural traditions, rough music in Sussex did not survive the Great War.

THE VILLAGE INN AT BURPHAM

The George and Dragon at Burpham stands beside one of the largest and best known earthworks in Sussex. It is a matter for speculation when or [by] whom these mounds were thrown up, but they were made in the days when man had no better tools than the shoulder-blade of an ox for a shovel and the antler of a red deer for a pickaxe. This earthwork is 317 yards long, 27 yards wide at the base and 7 yards high, which will give some idea of the gigantic task that was performed. It was made to protect the inhabitants from the north. The area of the field enclosed is 18 acres, which was formerly surrounded by water on the other three sides, thus making it an impregnable fort.

Although there is not much to say about the house, it is particularly remarkable that the inn was kept for 300 years by the West family who were noted in the past for their size and strength. The inn was owned by them until overtaken by bad times, when it was sold to the brewers. The family also had the village blacksmith's shop for a very long time. The Wests did not rely on the inn for a living, but kept horses and carts and hauled flints off the hills and loaded barges all year round.

In 1862 some of the Wests came into their own when the railway was being built in the Arun valley and the new cut of the river was being dug by hand to get material to lift the railway. Hundreds of men were brought from Lincolnshire to push the large navvy barrows, and it was among these that three of the Wests were put to work. This did not please the men from the north, who did all they could to drive them away at first, but on finding that they were more than equal to themselves, and that they owned the inn, they became the best of friends.

At this time the house was filled with gypsies, Irishmen and others come for the harvesting and John West had to stay at home. When he heard a quarrel in the tap room, he would walk in and order quiet and holding up his great fist would say "Remember, that's sudden death." That was usually sufficient warning, but on one occasion he was seen removing two struggling delinquents - one under each arm, to finish their quarrel outside. Many will remember George West, the last of the line, who died a bachelor. He was a good sportsman and very popular. After his death his two sisters carried on the inn until 1940.

First published in the *West Sussex Gazette*, 3 May 1956

It is known that the large earthwork referred to in the article was constructed during the reign of Alfred the Great, or his successor, Edward the Elder. That would make it eleven hundred years old at least. It was one of a series of forts, built to defend the south of England against the violent raids of the Vikings. The success of the resistance led to Burpham becoming an important stronghold, one which ranked with both Chichester and Lewes. These forts were known in Old English as "burghs", hence "Burpham", the home or farm by the fort. Later on in English history we get the "burgess", being a property-owning citizen of a town with "borough" status.

Had it not been for the Normans, who chose to build a new town at Arundel, thereby subverting the status of Burpham, the village could today be a bustling town with a castle and cathedral! The burgh is an important archaeological monument, which has been excavated on several occasions, most recently in 1972 and 1994.

When the writer John Cowper Powys came to Burpham in 1902, he moved into a house that backed onto the earthwork. At first he was delighted by the seclusion of his new rural retreat, but then became alarmed when he realised that he was being overlooked by the village children, playing on the burgh. Writing in 1934, Cowper Powys was able to reflect with humour on his early, futile attempts to keep the locals away:

> "Thus as time went on, being resolved at all costs to have the privacy of my small retreat intact, I caused a gigantic board, inscribed "Trespassers will be Prosecuted", to be erected on the top of the fortification. The village of Burpham awoke one morning therefore to find its historic rampart transformed overnight into the private property of an impecunious lecturer. The indignant natives acted at once. Certain among their bolderspirits, leaving their beer-mugs at the "George and Dragon", which was conveniently hard-by, transferred my board to a neighbouring ditch, where its threats of prosecution could be innocuously addressed to snails and slugs and field-mice. Once more was it replaced; only to be once more removed to the ditch.""

Today, wealthy incomers into a village expect privacy, and it is not unusual for footpaths to be diverted to suit their needs, but a century ago, John Cowper Powys' attitude was not appreciated. Perhaps he was lucky not to have got some rough music?

It is hard to prove that the West family had continuous ownership of the George and Dragon for the three hundred years up until 1940. Not until 1841 did a national census take place which gave details of name, address, age and occupation. In that year William West, aged 55, was residing at the inn and was named as the publican. There were seven other Wests listed as living there also, the oldest of these being Charles West, 30, whose given occupation was "bargeman". In Graburn's article, it is stated that the Wests supplemented their income from the inn with other work, including loading "barges all the year round".

There is a curious discrepancy between the 1881 and 1891 census returns. In the first year, John West, 38, is listed as the publican. Also listed is his wife, Mary, 38. Their children are listed, including, George, 15, and Ada, 13. George went on to be the last male West to be landlord. Ada, along with her sister, "Gurt", were the two sisters who gave up the inn in 1940, by which time Ada would have been 72. However the 1891 census, while listing George West, and giving his age as 25 as we would expect, gives his mother's age as 37, and there is no mention of the father. Presumably John had died in the interim, as Mary is named as the publican. If the 1881 census was correct, her age in 1891 should have been 48, not 37. If the 1891 census was correct, she was only twelve years old when she gave birth to George! Was the mistake with the enumerator, or did Mary West decide to knock off a few years? Whatever the answer, it does show that "historical documents'" are not always reliable. Whereas the oral tradition, of which Laurie was such a fine practitioner, may when put to the test prove more reliable.

There are still people living in Burpham today who can remember Ada and Gurt at the George and Dragon. Some remember how one of the old sisters had a great goitre on her neck, and cut a conspicuous figure. Others recall the habit the sisters had of blowing the froth off the top of the beer after they had finished pulling the pint into a jug. In 1967, it was reported in the Evening Argus that the Wests still exerted an influence over the pub they ran for so many generations. The then landlady, Peggy Briggs, still had a portrait of Ada West hanging in the bar, but she added that was not the only reminder of the Wests' legacy. "Occasionally things move," she told the Argus reporter, "perhaps a door opens or a window slams, when it happens we say 'that's Ada'. We say it partly as a joke, partly seriously. You never *know.* [8]

Today, pub landlords, often married couples, take over a house for six or seven years, then move on. In the past, the licence could remain with the same family for several generations, in much the same way as a shepherd or a blacksmith might inherit his trade from his father. There was a good deal less scope for ambition and financial advancement in the past, so it is hardly surprising that such a continuity existed, for what else was a man to do, other than follow the occupation of his father? Although the three-hundred year claim made for the Wests was exceptional, there were other families that ran local pubs for several generations.

When the Locomotive Inn was opened at Lyminster in 1846, its first landlord was George Mills. His daughter married James Mariner, who became the landlord on the death of his father-in-law in 1886. Later James' son took over, and when he died, the licence passed to his widow, who retired in 1961 - ending an uninterrupted family occupancy of 115 years. [9] In more recent times, the Cricketers at Broadwater was in the possession of the Medlock/Page family for 105 years. Following Wilf Page's death in 1988, the family reluctantly decided to relinquish the licence. It seems highly unlikely that these records will ever be broken. At the time of writing, Mervyn and Daphne Cutten, landlords of the Murrell Arms at Barnham since 1964, are probably the longest serving licensees in West Sussex.

JACK UPPERTON'S GIBBET, BURPHAM

Many have been anxious to know the exact position of Jack Upperton's gibbet, and as probably not more than half a dozen people living know where it stood, it has been suitably marked by an iron post with the initials "J.U.1771".

To anyone approaching Burpham from the direction of Arundel, by way of Blakehurst lane, two gates will be seen leading into the woods; proceeding 30 yards north from there, and leaving the gates on one's right hand, it can be seen in a clearance on the left.

Until 1868 the site was well marked by the stump of the old gallows tree, which remained until the late 1850s, and there-afterward by a large hole. The hole was then filled up after Lord Leconfield's huntsman's horse trod in it, giving the huntsman a nasty fall.

The crime for which Jack Upperton was hanged was attempted robbery of the mail which William Baldry was carrying on horseback, probably to or from Steyning. There were two men in the attempted hold-up, and old Burpham men have always said the worse offender of the two got away. It is not known from what house in Burpham Upperton went on that fateful night, and it is possible that he "laid about rough" as was the custom for many in those days. Anyway, the Vicar of Burpham must have claimed him, or he would not have ridden horseback to Lewes to visit him in jail.

According to some notes on Burpham, the Vicar said how sorry he was to see him in so serious a plight. To which Upperton replied "it was a scrambling sort of turn-out." (The word "scrambling" is still used locally by old people, meaning a muddled affair.) He was sentenced to death at East Grinstead, and I quote the words of the Judge, Baron Perrett: "and afterwards let him be hung in chains on the most convenient spot on Burpham New Down in the parish of Burpham, nearest to the gate at the end of Blakehurst lane Nr. Arundel in the County of Sussex."

The Judge's sentence conformed with the custom of those times which was that the criminal should be gibbeted at the most suitable place close to the scene of the crime. The spot chosen was probably bare downland at the time, but it is now covered by hazel and birch, which has encroached from the woods.

The blacksmith received £5 for making the iron and chains, which were necessary to prevent the friends or relatives from cutting down the body. On the first Sunday after he was gibbeted, all Burpham was there, with their families complete, taking a morbid interest in the horrid spectacle.

First published in the *Sussex County Magazine*, November 1957

In another article, published in the West Sussex Gazette *in 1959, Lawrie wrote of the loneliness of the woods where the gibbet is found, and of how walkers could easily get lost in the woodland still known to this day as "Gibbet Piece":*

A well-known writer once visited the spot at midnight, when it was full moon, and has described the eerie feeling of stillness and loneliness he felt while he was there, and he was glad to get away, although he had been through darkest Africa.

A Burpham man told a story that took place about 80 years ago. After his day's work, he was cutting wood for himself near the gibbet, of a March evening between the lights. He had just finished when he heard several people approaching, and stood still in the underwood. A little party of men and women stopped close to him, and an elderly man said, "Somewhere just near here is where the last highwayman was hung in chains, and it is said his ghost walks these paths at night." Whereupon the man shouted, "And here he is, too!" Never before had he seen a party bolt so quickly.

Numbers of people have been lost in the wood. Some have had to stay there all night and some have been found by searchers. There is a most remarkable case of a lady who can describe vividly being lost - and found - near the gibbet 78 years ago. She is Mrs. George Campbell, of Littlehampton, who was one of the large family of Mr. Robert Elliot, who lived at and farmed Angmering Park. When she was a child, it was the custom for a young governess to take the children of the family in the wood for a walk, and on one occasion his little girl became lost. No alarm was given at once, as it was thought she had run home. But when the party got home without her, in the failing light, immediate steps were taken to organise a search. All the farm staff turned out with lanterns, and shouts were heard all over the wood. But the little girl had walked away from home and reached the gibbet over a mile away.

She can still remember standing at the edge of the wood, crying and very frightened, and watching her tears drop into the water in a cart rut. Luckily a shepherd boy heard her crying, and when he heard she was lost and who her father was, he took her towards her home. It was by then pitch dark in the wood, and they had not gone far when they heard the shouts of the searchers. It was a great relief to her parents when they heard the shepherd shout, "I got 'er!".[10]

Graburn wrote several articles in the West Sussex Gazette *and elsewhere on the history and the legend of Jack Upperton. The historical facts are these: Upperton, a Burpham labourer over sixty years of age, robbed the post-boy, as he was bringing the mail over the Downs to Arundel. He was later arrested and tried at the Assizes, where he was sentenced to hang. After the execution at the notorious "Horsham Hang-Fair", Upperton's body was gibbeted, that is to say hung up in irons, at the scene of his crime. This was a common punishment for notorious criminals, such as murderers, smugglers and highwaymen. Not that it did much good, for although the punishments were severe in those days, the times were hard, and some people were prepared to take their chances. Also, there was no professional county police force, so the chances of being caught, in the short-term at least, were pretty slim.*

For some years, Jack's mouldering body, swung dismally on the gibbet pole near Blakehurst. Travellers on a dark winter's night would hear the bones rattling against the iron cage, and wish themselves to be in Arundel as soon as possible. For the country people living at Burpham, Wepham and Warningcamp, the gibbet was a familiar sight, but not one they were ever comfortable with. In one of his articles, Graburn told of the villagers' first viewing of the fearful spectacle, as related to the Rev. Robert Foster, who was vicar of Burpham for 53 years during Victorian times. The old people told Foster how the whole village had turned out to see Upperton's body hoisted up onto the gibbet one fateful Sunday. One old shepherd, looking up at the corpse, mused, "Ah, Jack, if you'd gone straight you wouldn't be a 'anging there now."[11]

Gibbeting took place all over Sussex, particularly in the eighteenth century. To this day "Jacob's Post" still marks the spot on Ditchling Common where Jacob Harris was gibbeted in 1734. Harris had broken into a nearby pub with the intention of robbing the place, but he roused the inhabitants from their sleep. In quick succession he murdered the maid, the pub landlord, and his bed-ridden wife. Right up until the late nineteenth century, poor people, living in the vicinity believed that a splinter of the gibbet post would act as a talisman against ill health. This curious belief was found in different forms elsewhere in Sussex.

At Rye in 1743, a town butcher by the name of John Breads murdered Alan Grebell, the deputy mayor. His intended victim had been James Lamb, the mayor, but in the dark, Breads had mistaken Grebell for Lamb. He ambushed him as he walked through the churchyard on his way home, carrying out the deed with a long, sharp butcher's knife. Breads was probably mad. At his trial (where James Lamb was the judge and jury!), he shouted across from the dock: "I didn't mean to kill him, I meant to kill you!" After being hanged, Breads was gibbeted. Old people in Rye were convinced that one of his bones, prised out of its irons, would work as a great cure for the rheumatics, and such bones were passed down through the generations.

The last men gibbeted in Sussex were probably two highwaymen, the Drewitt brothers, who were gibbeted near Fittleworth in 1799. The body of one of the brothers could still be seen four years later, until it was brought crashing to the ground during a gale: the remains were buried where they fell. So ended a gruesome chapter in the judicial history of the county. [12]

With Jack Upperton, it was his ghost, rather than his gibbet or mortal remains, which continued to excite the imagination of the public. At one time it was commonly believed that Jack's spirit haunted the woods. Two London gents, staying at Arundel in the 1920's were once enticed to the spot by locals keen to play a trick on these two "Bertie Wooster" types from the city. On reaching the gibbet on a rain-swept and blustery October evening, one of them, far from sober, swaggeringly enquired, "Well how are you tonight Jack?". When a voice answered back in solemn tones, "wet and cold! wet and cold!" the two young men fled from the spot as quickly as possible. My informant for the story assured me that "they were last seen headin' out for Chid-ester - 'undred miles an hour!" [13] *Such tales were told as much to demonstrate the gullibility of the Londoner and the guile of the Sussex countryman, as they were to prove the existence of Jack's ghost.*

As Graburn noted, woodland had grown over the Downs north of Blakehurst since Jack's robbery, and by the twentieth century these woods had become dense and forbidding. Graburn mentioned the writer who had journeyed in "darkest Africa", and yet still felt ill at ease in these woods. This was almost certainly Sir Harry Johnston, the colonial administrator, who was the uncle of Graburn's wife. John Cowper Powys also wrote about the woods, and his frequent walks through them, where he never met "a living soul". This however appealed to him, and he was glad that Jack Upperton's "indignant spirit seemed to keep people away from the spot." [14]

In 1951, Lawrie Graburn decided to put up a permanent memorial to the gibbet. In his journal entry for 15 May he wrote:

This afternoon G Hayler and I with a horse and cart to take material have marked the site of Jack Upperton's Gibbet, few people knew the exact spot, we were both shown it by J Holland, who in 1868 filled the hole after Lord Leconsfield's huntsman had a fall through his horse putting its foot in the hole where the 'Gallows Tree' had rotted away. The mark is an iron standard with an oak board neatly carved by Mr. Moody of Burpham (an artist) affixed with the letters J U 1771 and a gallows. [15]

This post and plaque stood for many years, until it was "lost", either through vandalism or as a result of pipe-laying in the area. It was replaced by a new plaque and post by members of the Upperton family, although Rosamund Hoy believes this to be in the wrong place, and is keen that it should be re-erected at the correct spot. She

said the motorist, opening the door and getting back into the driving seat.

Mark puffed at his pipe for a bit, looking thoughtful, and then said, "I want to ease your mind, Sir. Don't you sell that beautiful motor-car, or worry about the old dog any more. You've paid me very 'andsome, and to tell you the truth, I were takin' un' up to the copse to shoot 'un. 'Es gone blind and stone deaf. I dug a 'ole for 'un yesterday, so don't you worry no more. Good-mornin', Sir".

Producing an old bag from an inner pocket of his jacket, he put the dog in it, and shouldering his gun he trudged off up the road, without a backward glance at the very astonished motorist.

First published in the *West Sussex Gazette*, 1953

The "Silly Sussex" referred to in the article has an unexpected origin. Far from meaning that the people of the county are dim-witted, it is actually a toast of loyalty. Orginally, in Saxon times, it was "Saleag" Sussex, or "good-health" to Sussex. Such toasts would be made at banquets, or even amongst drinking companions at the village inn. Over the centuries its meaning and pronunciation have become obscured, leaving the perplexing boast of "Silly Sussex".

Graburn was a great admirer of Gray, and his famous Elegy. *In early 1941, shortly after the Battle of Britain, he pasted an extract from the poem into his scrapbook, writing in the margin, "Gray's wonderful prophecy over 200 years ago". This is the extract:*

> *The time will come, when thou shalt lift thine eyes*
> *To watch a long-drawn battle in the skies,*
> *While aged peasants, too amazed for words,*
> *Stare at the flying fleets of wond'rous birds.*
> *England, so long the mistress of the sea,*
> *Where winds and waves confess her sovereignty,*
> *Her ancient triumphs yet on high shall bear,*
> *And reign, the sovereign of the conquered air*

The story of Old Mark and his dog is of the type that always delighted Graburn, for it showed the countryman as stolid and imperturbable, and pretty shrewd when it came to money. In his journal Graburn refers to Mark and other old characters of rural West Sussex. Many of these anecdotes appeared in his articles: however some, probably considered too raunchy in the 1950's, did not. One of these unpublished tales concerned Old Mark, who at the age of 73 decided to get married. His lifelong friend expressed his surprise at the news, but suggested that his young wife might appreciate a lodger, as she was sure to get lonely, living in the isolated cottage. Shortly afterwards the friend became ill and had to go into hospital for some time. When he recovered and returned home he decided to see how Mark and his young wife were getting on. He found both of them well, and what was more, the wife was expecting a baby. He then enquired after the lodger, to which came the unexpected reply, "damned if she aint going to have one too"!

Mark and his associates were colourful characters and an essential part of the rural community. Graburn knew and liked these "rough diamonds", some of whom, as the following article suggests, lived at the margins of society.

HOW "RUNNERS" GOT A LIVING FROM THE LAND
Flints and Mushrooms

Changes in the countryside have swept away many old customs and quaint characters of the past. Early in this century and until the beginning of the first world war, we had many clever craftsmen visiting the Sussex villages. These men could re-seat chairs with rushes and cane, mend umbrellas, rivet china and sharpen knives and scissors. They could also make straw beehives. These were in great demand when cottagers kept one or two hives of bees. A hive of bees was always given to a young couple on their marriage. This was considered a handsome present, when honey was used to sweeten food before the introduction of sugar.

We also had another type of men called "runners", who got their living from the countryside in a different way. They arrived in April and like migratory birds, left in October. While they were in the country, they slept rough in hovels and earned money picking flints for the farmers on the hills, for which they received about a 1s per ton. This was a flourishing industry before the advent of the motor car, when thousands of tons of flint were drawn off the hills to repair the roads. But it was soon found that the sharp flints cut the tyres of motors. Tarmac was put on the roads instead, and the dusty highways and the flint trade disappeared.

These "runners", as the villagers called them, did not rely entirely on the flints for a living, but made use of anything that would earn them a little money. One old man, who came each spring, told me he came with the cuckoo, and that when he could tread on three daisies together, he could run - meaning, that when the daisies were thick he could always be sure of getting work. He started by picking cowslips, and then followed with kingcups which grew in profusion on the edge of a pond fed by clear spring water. These flowers he took to the seaside towns, where there was always a ready sale.

There was great rivalry between the runners, especially with mushrooms. On one occasion, one of them was digging potatoes for a man in the village. One morning he told his employer that he would not be there the next day before mid-day, as he had found a lot of mushrooms in Jim Holmes's field near the great woods which was a tidy step away, adding that they were just poking through and would be ready to pick if he went along at dawn the next day. His employer asked the man to bring him a few as he had not had any that year. Unfortunately there was a rival lying under the other side of the hedge, who heard the conversation, and not minding what hedge he slept under, made for the field at dusk and slept under some bushes nearby. He was up at peep-of-day and soon gathered over a bushel of lovely dewy mushrooms. The dawn was just breaking when he was on his way to sell his haul. Presently he met the enemy coming to the field, and seeing his look of angry astonishment at his basket filled to overflowing with mushrooms said, "You wants to get about in the mornin' for these things!"

The likeable old man who came with the cuckoo told us that his most lucrative week was when he found a patch of white heather amongst the purple of the Downs. It happened to be Goodwood Week, so he cut it all and made it into buttonholes. Then he took the train to Chichester where he met the race trains, the occupants of which changed to horse vehicles, which took them to the racecourse.

He told the people, "It aint no good looking up there without a bit o' luck, and I 'ave it 'ere for sixpence a sprig." Needless to say he did a roaring trade, and sold over 1,000 bunches. Unfortunately the white heather ran short, and there was no demand for the purple.

First published in the *West Sussex Gazette*, 20 October 1955

Bees played a crucial role in country life. Not only did they provide the only form of sweetener in honey, they also captivated the superstitious sense of the people. It was generally believed that if the head of the household died, then the bees must be told the sad news. If this was not done further calamities would follow: either there would be another death in the house, or, at the very least, the bees would leave.

Tickner Edwardes, long-time Burpham resident and future vicar of the parish, was a great bee-keeper. He wrote several books on the subject, one of which, The Lore of the Honey Bee, became a best-seller and still known to present-day bee-keepers. Edwardes sought to show how the traditions of the old bee-keepers, who used straw skeps, could be combined with the modern practitioners like himself, who used the wooden hives. In his journal, Graburn refers to both bee-keeping and the Rev. Edwardes, who gained much of his knowledge of bees from the old men in the village:

Joe Hoar who lived by the river was a pioneer and bought the hives of the first Duchess of Norfolk, the remains of which can be seen in the garden. He used to sell sections at 8d each and had about 30 stocks and looked after the bees at Peppering. Tickner Edwardes spent a lot of time with him before he wrote his "Lore of the Honey Bee" and would admit he learnt a lot from him. Old Joe told me when the book came out, "I knows as much as he does, but he knows how to make a book of it. And he will make more out of his book than he will selling honey."

In the early days, the bees had to be smoked out of the skeps, in order that the people could get the honey. Graburn's father remembered the fearless way in which the old bee-keepers dealt with the bees. Apparently, the more endowed you were with body hair the safer you were:

A Bee Keeper in Burpham of the old style was one David Butcher whose tomb can be seen just opposite the West Door [of the church]. Butcher was a farm worker and in the [18]60's my father was sent to see him one evening when he was taking honey. The bees were savage as is usual at this time, but Butcher was protected almost like a bear, with thick black hair on his chest and arms, and my father was much impressed by the way he kept pulling the bees out of his beard and the hair on his chest, completely ignoring their stings.

It was considered to be very lucky if a swarm of bees settled on a tree in your garden, and bitter disputes arose concerning ownership. Graburn recalled two old friends in the village who were engaged in a protracted dispute as to who was the rightful owner of a particular swarm. The case eventually came before the Arundel magistrates, who urged the men to settle their differences amicably. Such disputes often arose when the bees, kept in a skep by one man, swarmed and settled on another's property. Graburn recorded such an incident in his journal, concerning a Mr. Reed of Binstead who was able to reclaim his lost bees. The secret of success lay with the Queen Bee:

I saw Mr. Reed do the smartest thing I ever saw, he had imported some Italian queens as an experiment, and when I went there one day he showed me a very strong stock he expected to swarm, he had introduced an Italian queen into it. After watching it for a while we went to lunch, leaving his man to keep an eye on them. We had not been there long when the man came to say they had swarmed and were going away. Neither Mr. Reed or his man were very agile so I ran out and was able to follow them for a while, but could not keep up. The last I saw of them they were flying towards Dick Denyer's house. I reached this with no result when I met Mr. Reed just arriving, we then saw Denyer very excited, who told us a huge swarm had settled on a Plum tree in his garden. Mr. Reed assured him they were his bees, but Denyer would not part [with them] as he had kept bees before and his sisters wanted him to start again. We then watched Denyer take them, and as often happens a few returned to the bough. Mr. Reed looked at a little cluster and quickly picked one off and put it in a match box. He had the Italian queen and in a few seconds the air was full of bees again , and Mr. Reed told Denyer he would have to take them again, but they would not stay as he had the queen in his pocket. The bees not finding the queen returned to their old hive, and Denyer very upset at losing them.

The picking and selling of wild flowers is of course now illegal, but, as the article suggests, it was widespread in the early twentieth century. One man who strongly objected to this was Sir Harry Johnston, Mrs. Graburn's uncle, who lived at Poling Priory. In his autobiography, published in 1923, he launched into a blistering attack on the gypsies, whom he blamed for the trade. It was while describing his garden at Poling that Sir Harry made his accusations:

There are in addition, which I tremulously guard from tourist-raids, patches of wild Sussex daffodils - growing, increasing, multiplying, in our two Sussex orchards. I remember when I first took over this house and ground they grew in the farmers' meadows outside; they grew and blossomed deliciously in the Duke's woods across the road; grew throughout much of the landscape of Sussex. But about 1906 the accursed Gypsies, who, ever since, have been destroying the charm and colour of the Sussex landscapes for paltry gain, pounced on them in the woods and fields, dug them up, and wheeled them away to sell in Brighton, Worthing, Littlehampton and other mushroom places. The farmers raised not the slightest objection to the trespass or the despoiling. The only person besides myself who minded, or took any notice indeed, was the Duke's agent, who died on military service in the war."[16]

He goes on to say that the "gypsies" were not real Romanies, but itinerants from the East End of London who had married into gypsy stock. He also conceded that most people were not as hostile to them as he was, commenting that, "they are disliked by a few sensible old ladies, by myself, and by the Sussex police, who know them too well." Yet even the "real gypsies" (if indeed they ever existed) in the early nineteenth century were viewed with suspicion by many.

In 1849, gypsies at Ferring were arrested and charged with poisoning Farmer Trussler's pigs. It was stated that two gypsy women had asked for the corpses of the pigs shortly after they died. The farmer had refused the request and ordered the pigs to buried. Later however he discovered they had been exhumed. When the police raided the gypsy encampment, they found plenty of cooked and uncooked pork as well as a quantity of poison.[17] Interestingly of the five men arrested for the crime, three had the surname "Lee", a name commonly associated with gypsy families. Lawrie Graburn knew of this reputation, and in one of his articles he humorously explored the wariness people felt towards the "gypsies", combining this with a subtle understanding of human nature that underpinned so much of his observations and writings.

A view of the George and Dragon taken from the tower of Burpham Church.
Note the horse and Sussex waggon in the foreground.
Reproduced courtesy of West Sussex Library Service.

George West, landlord of the George and Dragon,
with a diverse "bag" of game.

"Stumpy" Arnold's cottage at Burpham. Burgh House now stands on the site.
Reproduced courtesy of West Sussex Library Service.

Roadknight's Post Office and General Stores (left), with George Goodyear's
(the wheel wright) house on the right.
Reproduced courtesy of West Sussex Library Service.

104 Wepham, home to Mervyn Peake during the Second World War. The
thatched roof was destroyed in a fire, and replaced by a tiled roof.
Reproduced courtesy of West Sussex Library Service.

Looking westward up The Street at Burpham. Today's transport in the village
is more likely to be four-wheeled drive than four-legged!
Reproduced courtesy of West Sussex Library Service.

Arundel Castle prior to the late Victorian re-building carried out by the 15th Duke of Norfolk.

Entrance to Wepham c. 1950s. The cottage on the left (now demolished) was the home of Charlie Roberts, renowned local poacher.

THE SQUIRE AND THE MUSHROOM PICKER
A country tale of sixty years ago

The squire had just finished breakfast, and was reading the morning paper propped up in front of him on the table. After a few minutes his eyes strayed to the long window, which gave a magnificent view of the park. He contemplated the spreading oak trees which were dotted about the lush meadows. Suddenly he gave a start of surprise. He could see a man with a basket, busily engaged in picking mushrooms, and being rather short-sighted he was unable to identity him. He rang for the butler and asked him to look out of the window and tell him if it was one of the estate employees.

"It is not a member of staff Sir," replied the butler after careful scrutiny, "but I think it is one of the gypsies from the camp at the end of the lane."

"Bring me my shoes, James. These people will be coming indoors next!" said the squire as he pushed back the chair. Then he walked to the window and watched the man, his temper rising as he saw the basket steadily filling with mushrooms.

"If I might say so, Sir," said James on his return with the shoes, "I should be cautious with the man. I heard that one of the tribe knocked a man down in the village last night and seriously injured him. He has been taken to hospital."

"What nonsense you do talk, James. Can't I speak to a man in the land of my birth? Land owned by my ancestors for generations?"

Having hurriedly put on his shoes, the squire crossed the hall and left the house by the side door. He then walked along the meadow and soon reached the man, whose back was turned to him. Apparently he was having a rest and was mopping his face and neck with a dirty piece of rag.

"You have no right here, my man, and I am going to take the mushrooms from you," said the squire, panting with the speed of his walk.

"No you ain't," replied the man, turning round. He was powerfully built, and of the gypsy type. He had visions of making a nice bit at the greengrocer's shop and did not relish giving up his haul. "There's plenty left for you," he added, fixing his black eyes on the squire. But seeing the determined look on his face said, "Who's land is this, Sir?"

"Mine," replied the squire.

"'Ow did you get it?" asked the gypsy, folding his arms.

"It was left me by my father," said the squire beginning to be amused.

"And 'ow did 'e get it?" said the gypsy, with a twinkle lurking in his eyes.

"It was left him by his father, and since you are so interested in my family I will tell you how they came by it. An ancestor of mine raised a troop of horsemen to quell a rebellion in Wales, and on his return he was granted this estate for services to king and country."

"Your family was all fighters then, Sir, and so were mine, but they didn't get no land give 'em. So lets you and me fight for these 'ere mushrooms."

"I am in no condition to fight as I have rheumatism in my neck and shoulder, nor do I want to call the police."

"That's right, Sir, we can settle this little matter without their 'elp."

"I would like some mushrooms for myself and my friends," said the squire, gazing thoughtfully at the white masses dotted about the field, "and I had no idea they were here in such quantities. It must be the agricultural salt I had sown here last winter."

"I'll fill you a basket or two, Sir, they want cutting as they are just right now."

"Very well," said the squire, as he walked off. "I'll send my man out with some baskets as I am going out later and would like to take some to my friends."

Reaching the house, the squire told James to take two baskets out to the man to fill. "Is he a very rough character?" inquired James. There was a suspicion of a quaver in his voice.

"His looks are the worst part of him I think," replied the squire. A smile lurked at the corners of his mouth as he watched James going off rather apprehensively to get the baskets.

An hour afterwards, while the squire was writing letters in his study, James came to say that the man had brought the mushrooms, and would like to speak to him.

"Show him in, James."

After a few minutes the door opened to admit the gypsy. "I've filled up they two baskets, Sir, and I thought you would like me to keep an eye on them mushrooms for a few days. You don't want a lot of rough 'uns there all day, and I could bring you as many as you want."

"That sounds a very good idea," said the squire, smiling, "as I expect the news has spread by now that there are a lot of mushrooms here. I shall leave you in charge to order off any intruders."

This pleased the gypsy, not being used to authority, and bidding the squire "good day" he went off.

Early next morning the squire was roused from a sound sleep by a familiar voice saying, "Get right out of 'ere. The squire don't want to look out of 'is winder and see a lot o' rough 'uns like you a-roaming` about. That's why 'e's put me in charge."

First published in the *West Sussex Gazette*, 12 August 1954

OLD NUTTER, A VILLAGE CHARACTER
Born under an Oak tree

About 100 years ago "Old Nutter", as he was called, was born in a village nestling at the foot of the South Downs and bordered on two sides by large woods. This remarkable man lived and died in the same village, hardly ever going further than Chichester, a distance of 13 miles.

Usually nicknames are started at school, but Old Nutter got his when he was a few days old and it stuck to him all his life. His father was a woodman who lived in a thatched cottage adjoining the large woods. On returning home one October evening, he was surprised to find that his wife was not there to greet him as was her custom. He asked a neighbour where she was and was told that she had gone nutting. He went into the wood and called her. After a short time he heard a faint answering cry. Following the sound he found his wife and newly born son under a large oak tree. He returned home for his wheelbarrow and brought them back safely, not forgetting the large basket of nuts his wife had collected. A few weeks later some woodcutters returning from work saw the mother and child in the garden of their cottage, and one of them called out to her "He's a nutter". So he was named for the rest of his life.

Nutter grew up to be a man of unusual strength and ability. He worked all his life in the woods where he was born, except for a few weeks in the summer when he joined the sheep shearers who went round the countryside to shear the large flocks of Southdown sheep which are now gone. When he was over 60 and had a grown family, he lost his wife. He then married again and reared a second family, some of whom were going to school when he died. One of these children got his father's nickname, but it was slightly changed to "Nutty".

At the time of his second marriage, Nutter gave up woodcutting and joined an old friend as rabbit and rat catcher all the winter. He was very proud of a letter he had received from a lady in a nearby village which said, "Dear Mr. Nutter, can you come to catch the rats in my poultry yard?" He kept this letter in an inner pocket of his coat and would show it to any stranger he met while having a pint in the village inn.

Nutter's mother attained a great age, and still lived in the same cottage where she had her family, and was looked after by a daughter. One April, a gang of oak tree fellers were working in the wood cutting down the trees and removing the bark, which was valuable for the tanning industry (this practice has now ceased as chemicals are used instead). As the gang passed the cottage they saw the old lady sitting by the window and one of them shouted, "We've cut that oak tree to-day, where Old Nutter was born." She waved her hand and smiled as she recognised one of her son's old school friends.

First published in the *West Sussex Gazette*, 23 May 1957

Old Nutter passed on many years ago, but the children from his second marriage are still alive. One of them, "Nobby" Kinnard still lives in Clapham, and until fairly recent years kept the wood-yard in France Lane, Patching. He is a fund of anecdotes and stories from the pre-war days, when the old crafts of hurdle-making and rabbit-catching were living trades.

Nobby, who was born in 1915, used to be taken rabbit-catching by his father. Nutter first took his son out when he was only eight: "We used to catch rabbits in the dark with 50' to 100' nets, which were four feet tall," Nobby recalls. "You had to have a good night, with the wind in the right direction, so your scent was not being blown in their direction. It was nothing to get fifty or sixty rabbits a night, and we could sell them for 9d each."

Nutter also taught Nobby to catch moles, and "all types of vermin", including rats. The moles were the most lucrative. A farmer would pay a lot of money for a moleskin waistcoat, but you needed to catch a lot of moles to make a waistcoat: "You'd catch them in 2lb jam jars," he remembers, "spring-traps were no good because they bruised the skins." Good skins would fetch up to sixpence, and between forty and fifty were needed for a waistcoat. Such were the ways that country people supplemented their income within living memory.[18]

Some people of course did not always seek permission before they helped themselves to the local wildlife, situated on private property. By the early nineteenth century, most of the common land had been enclosed, which meant all land had become private land. Poor families, if they wanted to have meat in their diet, depended on the nightly raids of poaching gangs. In the 1830's and 40's, these gangs fought pitched battles with gamekeepers, and there were casualties, including fatalities, on both sides. The harsh game laws meant that a convicted poacher could face transportation to Australia.

By the time that Graburn's father came to West Sussex in 1861, the condition of the labourers had eased. Although the well-armed gangs had gone, the individual poacher remained. These men were often semi-itinerants, or men with no stable employment, for whom poaching became a way of life. The following article by Graburn tells the tale of one such poacher, notorious in the days of his father and grandfather.

THE OLD POACHER

It was in November, 1873, that the old poacher was at last caught. He had been a continual trouble to the keepers on a large estate owned by a nobleman, for his clever tricks always defeated them.

At that time the rearing of pheasants was becoming popular, and a large wood with one public footpath through it was well known to the old poacher and an annoyance to the keepers. A favourite trick was to walk through it of a winter's afternoon smoking his little clay pipe (upside down) just when the pheasants were going up to roost.

One afternoon he saw two keepers step behind a holly, thinking they had not been seen. He went on slowly down the path, knowing he was being watched. Birds were going up fast, and he aimed at them with his stick, and then pulled it through the decaying beech leaves, leaving a mark, several times.

His friends in the holly went home to tea and came back prepared for a long wait - and they had it. The birds near the path had a good night's rest, a few in a copse a mile away died that night.

A ruse that pleased the old bricklayer-poacher more than any was when a neighbour, to whom he often gave a rabbit or a hare, told him a keeper and a policeman had been watching his house to see him return early in the morning.

"Thanks for telling me, I'll wait on 'em another day."

One morning early he was returning to his little thatched cottage with a few birds in a bag, and the neighbour's warning had made him work out a fresh plan. In a dry ditch about 300 yards from his home he had deposited a bag of small tins; these he shouldered, leaving the game safely hidden in the hedge.

He walked boldly down the village street, and met a carter going to feed his horses, who said: "You're about early today!"

"Yes, I likes to get about in the mornin'."

He had not gone far when he was confronted by the policeman and a keeper who had been hidden in a hedge. "What are you up to now?" asked the old poacher.

"I want to see what you've got in that bag !" said the P.C.

"You can see 'um, and hav'em, too," answered the old man, as he emptied the bag with a rattle on the road. When they were well clear he went back and got a more valuable sack.

There were many more of the old man's tricks which were told in the village, but all good things come to an end and he was caught after over twenty years by the keepers he had so often tricked in the past.

At the local court the new mayor sat for the first time. The case having been heard, the mayor asked the clerk to the magistrates what the fine should be, and told the old man, who at once said: "You wouldn't like to starve three helpless women, yer honour; my old wife has the 'screws' so bad she can't walk, and my two daughters aren't right up top and can't go out to work."

The mayor talked to the clerk, who said he knew of the daughters' disabilities but nothing of his wife's "screws".

The mayor then said: "As it is my first day on the bench I shall pay the fine myself." Thanking him profusely, and wishing him a happy Christmas, the poacher left the court.

Within six weeks he was back in the same place. This time there was nothing for it but a prison sentence. Hearing how many weeks he had to serve, the old man said to the mayor: "Let me stay at home, sir, and I'll bring you a brace of birds every week till the end of the season."

"Where do you propose to get these birds?" enquired the mayor.

After a moment's thought he replied: "I should have to buy 'em from Dick Groves who takes the game after the big shoots."

There was a happy sequel to the old man's return. While sitting over the fire a few days later with his wife and two daughters, there was a knock at the door. The old poacher answered it himself. It was the nobleman, whose game he had so often poached in the past, who shook him by the hand and said: "I'm short of a good brick-layer, I wonder if you would come and take the job and give up poaching?"

"I will, Sir!"

They shook hands and he never poached again. And that is a true story, too.

First published in *The Gamekeeper and Countryside*, May 1958

In his journal, Graburn gives details omitted from the article. The poacher's name was "Lordy Finch" and the mayor who showed such forbearance towards him was Graburn's grandfather. He also tells of other local poachers, also known to his father:

Two more of these worthies lived in sheds in the Arundel brooks, their names I never knew, but they were known as "Nine Eyes" and "Billy Treadlight", both aptly named. These two were drovers, and at times had quite a lot of work moving cattle to fresh pastures and markets. But when big pheasant shoots were on the keepers looked to employ them as they then knew where they were.

My father saw the following episode outside the keeper's house at Upper Barpham: The guns had gone into the cottage for lunch, the Duke and Lord Edmund Talbot were shooting and Col. Mostyn was in command. All beaters and stops had lunch outside. While they were eating their lunch the Superintendent of the police drove up in his dog-cart with a constable. Treadlight knew he was suspected and watched, and retired to a cow shed where Nine Eyes proceeded to fill his huge poacher's pocket with sloppy cow manure, they then returned having stuck a cock pheasant's tail feathers in it. It was not long before a keeper pointed it out to Col. Mostyn who at once asked the Super to search him. This Treadlight resented, but seeing the feathers the Super made a grab, expecting to find birds - he was disappointed, his tunic to the elbow was covered with manure. All laughed heartily but no one louder and longer than Treadlight.

HURDLES AND HONEYSUCKLE
A Dying Craft

Walking through a wood recently, I came upon a man working at the ancient and dying craft of hurdle-making. He was grumbling about the honeysuckle. All wood workers hate it, as not only does it spoil many rods that would be put in a hurdle if they had not been made impossible to split through the honeysuckle growing around them; but it is a great nuisance to the men who cut the wood down.

Pointing to a lot of hazel sticks, he said, "Look at 'em. No good for nothin' except fireun'." He went on to say that the honeysuckle grew right into the sticks, but I ventured to point out that it grew round the stick so tightly that the stick grew over the honeysuckle. I showed a piece almost hidden, and he agreed with me, but added, "That don't make it no better, do it?"

There does not appear to be any other climber that marks a stick like honeysuckle, which always grows round the stick clockwise. Now runner beans grow round a pole anti-clockwise and nothing will induce either to grow the opposite way. An old man I know has tried for years to make a single bean grow the opposite way, but without success. Ivy grows both ways, but mostly clockwise.

Before the flocks of Southdown sheep were given up, hurdle-making was quite an industry, each farm wanting 15 to 30 dozen a year when folds were pitched every day. When the hurdles were made, they were stacked ten dozen in a lump in the woods, with ten dozen stakes on top and usually a good straight stick for the shepherd's crook, and they were sold for 9s. or 10s. per dozen before the first great war. Hurdles were always made by the dozen, the maker receiving about half the price fetched. Early in that war (when prices began to rise) a wood owner was paying his woodcutters and hurdle-makers at the end of the week and said to one hurdle-maker, "I see you've pretty well finished and you'll want a fresh job next week." "Not at this price I shan't," said the man. "What do you want now then?" "Six shillings per dozen," said the man. "You'll never get that as long as you live." But he got it the next week.

Many years ago a Hampshire hurdle-maker appeared in these parts, and the news went round that he could make two dozen hurdles in a day, one dozen always being considered a good day's work in Sussex. The hurdle-makers who went to see him agreed he was very fast, but said he did not put in the same amount of work as they did. The man did not stay long, having several employers before returning to Hampshire.

My first experience of hurdles was being sent as a boy on a pony to the wood merchant to tell him that the hurdles that had been ordered were badly wanted. On my way I passed the shepherd and told him where I was going. He said, "Tell him not to put a lot of withy in the hurdles this time. They won't last a twelve month." This I was pleased to do, and when I quoted the shepherd's words, the man looked at me and said, "I should think very likely you're a better judge of a beef steak puddun' than you are of a hurdle." I went home rather subdued.

Many of the old hurdle-makers are resting in the churchyards at Clapham, Patching and Angmering, near the big woods where they worked so long.

First published in the *West Sussex Gazette*, 20 December 1956

Nobby Kinnard and his men continued to make hurdles at Patching until the 1970's, by which time the demand for them had almost gone. They also made wattles, often confused with hurdles, but actually quite different. A hurdle is made of split hazel roads, while a wattle is more like a gate or fence in its construction. Wattles were in particular demand for the folding of sheep on the Downs, something that was a common sight until the Second World War. One of Nobby's last jobs was to supply wattles for the Findon Sheep Fair, held annually on Nepcote Green since at least the eighteenth century.

For over two hundred years the "Wattle House" has stood on the Green. It was purpose built around 1790, specifically for storing the wattles between fair days. At various times people did make their homes in the upper stories, including on one occasion the village postman.

By the early nineteenth century the Southdown breed of sheep predominated on the hills of Sussex. The breed, noted for the quality of both its wool and meat had been perfected by John Ellman of Glynde, who cross-bred sheep for many years until he produced what he believed was the ideal sheep. Southdowns were exported right across the British Isles and across the British Empire. At one time it would have been hard to find a Sussex farmer or shepherd who had experience of any other breed.

In recent years, the Findon fair has been in decline. The price of sheep has fallen, and Southdowns are now a rarity. In days when consumer pressures demand "good value", the Southdown has lost out, for although its quality remains high, other sheep, which grow larger and produce more lambs, are now the chosen option. During the 1990's it was even doubted if the sheep fair at Findon could continue, as so few flocks were been entered for the sale. Modern regulations forbade the use of wattles for folding sheep, and metal ones had to be used instead. The amusements fair, which had long accompanied the sheep sale, became the bigger attraction. There was even talk of the Wattle House being demolished, and not everyone was pleased when it was designated as a "listed" building.

By 2000, however, the fair was enjoying a revival under the auspices of an enthusiastic committee, dedicated to its future as both a sheep and an amusements fair. Today live music has been added to the evening's entertainment, and throughout the day stall-holders offer their wares and services. Findon Sheep Fair has been evolving over the decades, and as the following article demonstrates, Graburn noted changes at Nepcote during his lifetime.

Sheep-washing by Herman, early 1900s. Note the men standing in the barrels, coaxing the sheep through the dip.

Splash Farm with cattle, and Arundel castle in the distance. Painted by H. C. Fox in 1914.

The old river-crossing at Burpham painted by Herman.

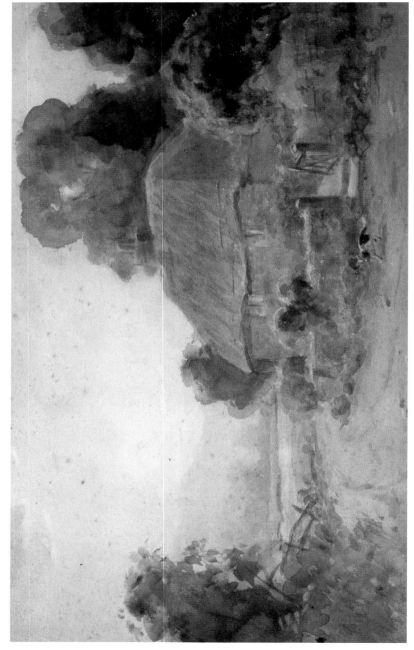

"Stumpy" Arnold's Cottage by unknown artist. Burgh House stands on the site today. The lane leads to The Splash.

Herman's painting of the George and Dragon before the First World War, in the days when George West was landlord.

A view across corn stooks to Burpham Church. Painted by Herman in 1915, shortly before the German-born artist was interned as an "enemy alien".

CHANGES AT FINDON FAIR IN 55 YEARS
Bargains before the days of the auctioneer

If an old farmer, who last saw Findon Fair in 1898, could see it as it is to-day, he would, I think, notice three things in particular. First, the auctioneer, who did not appear at the fair until several years after this date. Secondly, the various breeds of sheep; it was Southdowns only at that time. And thirdly, the large double-deck transport vans used to take the animals from the fair. All the sheep, except the rams, walked to the fair in 1898, some taking two days to get there. The rams in most cases arrived in Sussex wagons, with hurdles round them.

This same farmer, or shepherd, would not fail to remember the hush and quietness when the fair began. Farmers looking at lambs would ask in a whisper what the owner was going to take for his best. Many farmers had no idea what to ask until some were sold, the first lots fixing the price. A dealer would say, "Good morning, Mr. ----, what are you asking for your best 100 wether lambs?", the farmer replying, "44s. apiece." The dealer would answer, as he walked away, "You haven't been to any fairs this summer, I can see. I'll come round and see you later in the day, when you are a little more educated."

The big flockmasters sold their lambs and ewes 100 in a pen; it is now never more than 50. When the first deal was made, a shout would go up "sold again", and there was quite a rush to see the sheep, and to find out the price they had made. This was accompanied by a shrill whistle from an engine in the pleasure fair, which did not start until the sheep fair was over. The arrival of the auctioneer was a great help to the farmers, although he was opposed for a long time, and did not get established for several years. Many old farmers never made the change.

At the time of which I am writing there was a cycle of hot and dry summers. Sheep-feed was scarce and flockmasters had a hard time with dry ponds, water carting for long distances and the sheep fetching such low prices at the end. Best wether lambs made 32s. to 38s. and regular draft ewes 37s. to 42s.

The farmers arrived at the fair in dogcarts, or rode over the Downs on horseback. Gaiters (now hardly ever seen) were the fashion for farmer and shepherd, and were worn even if it was a very hot day.

From the spectators' point of view, the fair was much more interesting than it is to-day. There was always a drove of Irish or Welsh colts, which late in the day would be ridden and jumped and, as the beer flowed more freely, would be put in carts and driven. There were also quite a number of Irish and other cattle, which were sold after the fair was over.

The biggest sender of sheep was Mr. Charles Duke, of Lee Farm, the last of the Dukes, who farmed that farm for 200 years. He had, at this particular fair, 1,000 ewes and lambs. Heavy rains having come before the fair, the trade was better than expected and Mr. Duke had sold his last pen of lambs by 3 o'clock, and was walking with a neighbour to the village to get his horse, when an Irishman stopped him and said, "Will you buy this good lot of heifer calves, yer honour?" Mr. Duke, having made a few hundreds more for his sheep than expected, glanced at the calves and said, "How much?" The man replied, "£5 apiece." "Give you half," said Mr. Duke and, increasing his bid by 2s 6d a head, was the owner of 70 calves. People thought they must have been stolen to be sold at such a cheap price, as they were fine cattle.

The deal was a disappointment to Mr. Duke's shepherds and boys when he found them in the pleasure fair, because they had to leave and drive the calves back to

Lee Farm. The pleasure fair was kept up until late hours. People came in from the surrounding villages to spend the evening.

The first lot of sheep other than Southdowns was sold at Findon a few years later. They were penned at the lower end of the fair by themselves and had hurdles on end round them to stop them jumping. All the shepherds were very interested in them. One old shepherd was heard to say, "I'm going to look at these wild sheep down here. They say they've got horns and long tails, and they caught 'em on the mountains in Wales." The old man quite believed they were wild sheep, never having seen any sheep other than Southdowns.

Most of the lambs were bought by farmers from the coast-land, hill-bred lambs always being in demand. Thousands were fattened on roots every winter.

It seems strange to think that folded sheep on the land were called the "golden hoof" and it was thought they could not be done without. Now folding sheep is almost unknown. The sheep of to-day are nearly all grass sheep, and the Southdown flocks and bells and the shepherds on the Downs are gone for ever.

First published in the West Sussex Gazette, 10 September 1953

Two writers, resident in Burpham, highlighted the annual sheep washing as a red-letter day in Burpham before the First World War. John Cowper Powys wrote: "The great event of the year at Burpham was the sheep-washing which took place in a narrow estuary of the river. Early in the morning a vast continuous stream of woolly sheep would pour down the lane past our house, filling the whole space between the walls, and making a peculiar sound unlike anything else."[19] Powys went on to add that, "Mr. Edwardes in his role as a writer of nature sketches was always on the scene." It is to Tickner Edwardes we must turn for a vivid impression of those far-off days:

"The shepherds, the washing-gang, the little crowd of onlookers, are lounging on the green river-bank, chatting idly together as if there were no more weighty business in hand than to enjoy the summer morning. The dogs are mostly asleep on their chains. Only the old captain of the wash is astir. He roves about, here tightening up a girth in his tackle, and there straightening a crooked hurdle; and every minute or two he goes and looks over the plunge, measuring the depth of the water with his eye. At last he gives the signal, every man goes to his post, and the silence of the old quarry breaks as with the crash of a sudden storm. For it is nearly impossible to convey a real idea of the hubbub and turmoil of the scene under any less decided simile. From the moment the first sheep is thrown in, until the last terrified, bedraggled ewe staggers up the slippery incline at the other end of the creek, there is one long, unceasing babel of sound. Often a score of sheep are in the water at the same time, each one rending the air with her piteous calling. Those that have passed through the ordeal crowd together on the beach above, still lifting to the skies their mingled note of indignation and alarm; and those as yet dry in the great pen anticipate their sufferings with a like deafening tumult. The yapping chorus of the dogs punctuates the entire symphony; and every man engaged in the work joins in a general running fire of comment and mutual encouragement, although hardly any sound less forceful than the bellow of a bull can be heard above the din."[20]

The decline in sheep-farming was hastened by the advent of the Second World War, when the Downs were either given over to the plough as part of the "Dig for Victory" campaign, or else became a military training zone. After 1945 the military left, but the sheep never returned. In his journal, Lawrie noted the changing scene, as he sat on the Downs near Storrington one summer's day in 1947: "I then pictured the downs as I knew them 40 years before, the change now is remarkable. The downs then were cropped short as a lawn by a flock of Southdown ewes, each tended by a

Shepherd or boy with no wire fences as now."

The change had been so sudden and so complete that there was little opportunity for public concern to be expressed. An earlier generation would have been astonished. Writing in the early years of the twentieth century, the naturalist W. H. Hudson had confidently predicted that, "the solitary shepherd with his dog at his feet will doubtless stand watching his flock on the hillside for some thousands of years to come."²¹

DEATH OF A SHEPHERD

In a hamlet north of the South Downs there is a thatched cottage with a history. Experts examining the old timbers and walls have said that it is 15th century. Some of the timbers in the house must have been growing before William the Conqueror reached these shores, and they are cut with an adze, a tool seldom used to-day.

A large hook fixed to one of the beams still remains, where many a fat hog hung before being cut up and put into pickle in a slate tank for the oxman and shepherd. They lived in each end of the cottage, which in its early days had been a farmhouse occupied by one family.

The shepherds from this cottage had been making a considerable income catching wheatears, as the down where they tended their 500-ewe flock was the assembly ground before migration for these small birds. Gourmets of the time would have them at any price.

One old shepherd had many customers in the district, and although he caught large numbers of wheatears, with the aid of horsehair nooses, he found it difficult to satisfy their appetites for these dainty morsels. When the house was sold 112 years ago, it came as no surprise to people who knew shepherd Arnold to hear he had bought the cottages and land for £180 cash. He kept his money in an iron box in a hole in a large beam, and every penny in it was profits from catching wheatears, from August until they left these shores.

Old Arnold had reared a large family of two sons and five daughters. The two sons were also shepherds, and the two single daughters looked after the old man when he retired, his wife having died several years before.

These daughters did not have an easy task, as their father's temper, after he was 85, was very uncertain, and he became bedridden.

One day he asked to see his old friend George Goodyear, the wheelwright and undertaker. His daughters thought it a very good idea, as it would cheer him up. They called on George and fixed the day for the visit.

When George came he had difficulty in climbing the stairs, and sat for some time without speaking. Old Arnold said: "You 'aven't got much news, now you 'ave come."

"I'm a thinkun it will be a tidy old job for someone gettun a coffin down they twisty stairs," said George. "They be as crooked as a dog's 'ind leg."

"Ah! you never started thinkun soon enough, George," said the old shepherd.

"It do seem a tidy puzzle," replied the undertaker, scratching his head.

"I tried to get a six-foot board in 'ere when I could get about, and couldn't, let alone a coffin. That's why I sent for you," said Arnold, looking severely at his friend. "Now when your sons are sawing out some elm boards at the saw-pit, I want them to saw out a couple of elm slabs about 3 feet long and 2 inches thick, then come back and knock a hole in the wall at floor level and then nail them over the 'ole."

A few days later the work was carried out, watched with great interest by Arnold. He shouted out: "Don't ram they boards on too tight. They'll 'ave to come off again afore long."

Some months later the old man died, and all his children and their families came for the funeral. The eldest son brought a lock of wool to put in the old man's hand in the coffin. This ancient custom was, of course, to show the man's calling, and to excuse him to his maker for absence from divine service over the years.

The boards were then removed and the coffin was slid down the plank on to the shoulders of the bearers, who had a two-mile walk to the church where he was buried.

So the old shepherd made his last journey down the long winding lane he had used for over 80 years. The elm slabs were nailed on again that night, and are still to be seen to-day.

First published in the *Farmer and Stock-Breeder*, 24 September 1957

Shepherds were renowned for their self-reliance and imperturbability. The same appears to have been true for the Arnold family as a whole. Graburn wrote that they were very hard workers "that farmers only dream of". The last of the line, Jack Arnold, had a leg amputated as a young man, after which he was always known as "Stumpy" Arnold. Yet he remained a hard worker: "When well over 70 he set out 10 acres of Swedes in a fortnight," Graburn recorded.

The catching of wheatears by shepherds on the Downs was well documented by nineteenth-century writers, who blamed the shepherds for the bird's decline. Certainly it is rarely seen today, but to the shepherd's of the time it was an important source of extra income, and one not to be missed. By the time W. H. Hudson was writing Nature in Downland, in 1899, the bird was virtually extinct from the South Downs. Hudson recalled previous generations "looked on the eating of wheatears as the highest pleasure man could know." He also went on to describe the method of their capture:

"In July the shepherds made their "coops", as their traps were called - a T-shaped trench about fourteen inches long, over which the two long narrow sods cut nearly out of the turf were adjusted, grass downwards. A small opening was left at the end for ingress, and there was room in the passage for the bird to pass through towards the chinks of light coming from the two ends of the cross passage. At the inner end of the passage a horse-hair spring was set, by which the bird was caught by the neck as it passed in, but the noose did not as a rule strangle the bird."

According to Hudson, the birds were especially attracted to the coops on days of broken cloud, when sunshine was constantly being exchanged for shade; this he thought was due to the birds dislike of rain, which they associated with the "sudden gloom caused by a cloud obscuring the sun." On such days the shepherds would make regular visits to their traps, sure of a good catch. However on days of unbroken cloud or continuous sunshine, "he hardly thought it worth while to visit his coops".

THE DUKE FAMILY OF WEST SUSSEX
Tales of Farmers with a "streak of madness"

Until the end of the last century Duke was the commonest name in the farming world in West Sussex; farm after farm was occupied by a Duke. It was said 100 years ago that one could ride horse-back from Chichester to Steyning without riding off the land of a Duke. How strange that this huge clan should have disappeared so completely from the agricultural world, though the name is still common in the county. There was a streak of eccentricity and wildness in many of the family, as some of the following incidents taken from an old Duke diary will show.

From 1701 for 200 years Lee Farm, a large hill farm six miles north-east of Arundel, was farmed by the Duke family. The first record is of the one who farmed there just after the Napoleonic wars. He kept a large number of working oxen and 1,000 breeding ewes, and broke up a lot of land to grow wheat when corn was very dear. He had 14 children - eight boys and six girls - and made every boy a doctor. It is most likely that some of the "Doctor Dukes" of today could trace their ancestry to this man. At his death a nephew took over the farm.

Another Duke who farmed nearby at this time was noted for his size, appetite, and loud voice (like many other Dukes), and suffered terribly from gout. On one occasion, having a very bad attack, he sent for the doctor, who told him that he must give up port wine or it would kill him. To this he replied that it would kill him to give it up. He eventually agreed to cut down to a glass a day. This he found quite inadequate, so he ordered a glass to be made to hold a quart! I have this lovely glass in my possession and it rings like a bell.

Two young Dukes at this time, farming near Chichester, drove to a cousin's farm near Arundel for a day's coursing. Going to lunch, they met a wagon which had come from their farm loaded with seed corn, which they had sold to their cousin. They were struck by the number of boys watching the corn being unloaded. On making inquiry, they were told that there were three families with ten children or more. As they had no boys on their farm, they asked the foreman to approach the parents to see if they would part with one boy from each family. The parents readily agreed to this, as they found great difficulty in feeding and clothing so many children in those hungry times. The brothers assured the parents that the boys would be well taken for; one saying he had a lot of boys' clothing outgrown, and the other had a tank full of fat pork, and there was a widow to look after them.

When the wagon was about to start, one of the brothers insisted that the boys should be tied up in pokes so that they should not see their way home. The boys were happy and soon settled down, never to return to their old home. Such was life 130 years ago.

At a considerably later date an incident occurred which just escaped serious trouble. Another Duke had two sons, both very fond of sport. They asked their father, a few days before the Derby, if they could have the day off to go to the races. "Certainly not," was the reply, "with all that clover-hay cut, and ready to carry!" This was a keen disappointment to the young men, who, however, were determined to go.

Rising very early on Derby Day, they ran two of their father's fat bullocks to a nearby slaughterhouse and collected 40 sovereigns in cash and went to Epsom. They did not bet until the Derby, when they put half the bullock money on the winner. As the horses rounded Tattenham Corner, one brother said to the other "I never saw the old man's bullocks go so fast!"

At the end of the day they returned home in good spirits with a nice bit of cash. On reaching the farm they saw the last load of hay going into the rick yard. Rounding the house, they had a rude awakening as the Superintendent of Police was sitting in his dog cart in front of the house, and their father, decanter in hand, was pouring him out some whisky. How the affair was settled is not known.

There was another Duke, a great character, who riding to Goodwood Races was overtaken by the Duke of Richmond's coach. The Duke stopped and said, "Mr. Duke, some of my friends want to know how heavy you are."

"I weigh 24 stone and my horse weighs a ton," replied Mr. Duke. The latter statement was, of course, an exaggeration.

When 65 years of age, this huge man backed himself at an Arundel fat stock dinner to plough an acre in a day for a considerable wager. The day was fixed, and an acre measured out in front of Blakehurst farmhouse. Farmers rode and drove long distances to see the result of the wager, which was won by 3 o'clock.

Before bidding farewell to the Dukes, I would like to say that it is now known that Neville Duke (the intrepid airman) is one of this family.

First published in the *West Sussex Gazette*, 28 January 1954

As the old established families disappeared, so they were replaced by an exotic combination of writers, artists and academics. Firstly the railway to Arundel, then the "new road" to Burpham, enabled strangers to reach the village with comparative ease. Also, by the late nineteenth century there was a growing mood amongst many affluent, educated people that the cities and large towns were becoming vile places, dogged by crime, pollution and noise: the countryside offered an escape. It was quite possible for such literary personages to reside in Burpham, but be in easy reach of London, if they needed to consult editors and publishers. John Ruskin was a frequent visitor to Peppering, Tickner Edwardes came, stayed, and later became vicar. And amongst this visitation of painters, poets and novelists there came John Cowper Powys, a neurotic, even tortured genius, whose writings are enjoying something of a revival today.

As has already been mentioned in connection with the George and Dragon, Powys was not always popular with the locals, yet much of his aloofness arose from his own, painful shyness. He described coming upon a group of "Mr. Graburn's men, eating their meal in the harvest field", and that he was "so terrified that in dead silence", he "shuffled past them as if I had been a deaf-mute."[23] As well as expressing the respect he had for "Mr. Collyer and Mr. Graburn," the two local farmers, he also mentions their sons, stating, "They were youths of good parts and of charming presence but they were almost as shy of me as I was of them." One of these reserved young men was of course Lawrie Graburn.

Cowper Powys also mentioned other village characters who impressed him, including "Mr. Budd the blacksmith, Mr. Goodyear the carpenter, George West the landlord of the George and Dragon." Most of all he praised Mr. Roadnight, who ran the local stores, for being the great conciliator of village disputes, for being perhaps the man Powys himself would have liked to have been:

"The respect we had for this incomparable young man remains with me still as a most happy memory. With a smooth high forehead and a large ruddy clean-shaven face, with a choice and even meticulous manner of speech, George Roadnight played the part of benevolent Home Secretary to our small hamlet. A Liberal in politics he seemed to stand as the mediating focus-point between all the clashing

and contradictory forces of our little community. We all came to him; we all leaned on him; we all trusted him. I have never known in my life any human being so dedicated to take the right path in troubled waters. The side upon which George Roadknight was was always the right side."

Powys has left us some rather memorable descriptions of both the village and its surrounding countryside. Sometimes these descriptions reflect his own, melancholy thoughts, at other times it seems as if the village and its people are soothing his troubled soul, and raising his mood:

"All day long at Burpham there poured in upon us with the full flood of sunshine the voices of children, the bleating of sheep, the lowing of oxen, the ringing of bells, the stamping of horses, the tinkling of anvils, the sawing of timber, together with the most cheerful voices from the George and Dragon. We had so much sunshine in fact and such lively sounds in every direction that it seems strange that my proud and vicious loneliness was not melted, humanized, precipitated, made into a sweet savour of humility."[24]

Burpham today is mainly a village for people who are retired, or who work away, perhaps only coming to their houses there at the week-ends. One hundred years ago John Cowper Powys was a curious figure in the village, something of an isolated individual, surrounded by a tightly-knit community, which based itself around traditional farming practices while adhering to a strictly observed moral and social code. Such conformity and deference were deeply alien to this anxious writer

Fences and animal-feeders made out of hazel by Sussex hurdle-makers, such as the Kinnard family at Patching.

A flock of sheep by the River Arun at Burpham in about 1910.
Reproduced courtesy of West Sussex Library Service.

Bringing home the flock – a winter's day between the Wars.
Reproduced courtesy of West Sussex Library Service.

Sheep-dipping at Burpham – late nineteenth century.
Reproduced courtesy of West Sussex Library Service.

Sketch of Hare drawn by Agnes Graburn (1900–1984), Lawrie's wife.

A lark-glass lure.

A shepherd and his flock on a balmy summer's day. One of a series drawn for Mr. and Mrs. Graburn by Kirkpatrick.

Harrowing with horses. Kirkpatrick.

Ploughing with horses. Kirkpatrick.

One man, four horses and the open sky. Kirkpatrick.

GOODWOOD RACES BEFORE THE MOTOR CAR
When the course was free to all

When the great crowds go to Goodwood again this summer, there will not be many who went before the advent of the motor-car. One of the greatest improvements of recent times must be the tarred roads. Before this the traffic stirred up a fine white dust, which made the hedges look as if they were covered with flour, and people arrived on the course looking like millers - white from head to foot.

It was a fine sight to see the coaches arrive, and to hear the coach horns echoing in the woods, as they drove through the Birdless Grove. The gypsies did well with cart-horses fitted with rope traces to give a pull-up to heavily laden coaches and other vehicles. As soon as they had drawn up a coach or brake, they would gallop back bare-back to deal with another customer wanting assistance. There were huge tents to accommodate the hundreds of coach and carriage horses, as well as saddle horses which had been ridden over the Downs to the meeting. Special trains brought cabs and their horses down from London on the Sunday before racing. They stayed a fortnight in Sussex, then returned to London by road, taking about a couple of days on the journey.

In those days the racecourse was free to all. The bookmakers used the rails opposite the stands as well as the rings. The crowd poured on to the course between races to make their bets and to watch the many and varied side-shows. Tipsters, nigger minstrels, whip-crackers, games of chance were all to be seen. There was also a man on very high stilts, who walked among the coaches catching coins thrown to him with a top hat. This man on one occasion walked down the course until opposite the royal box, where he saluted King Edward, who seemed amused and acknowledged him. An equerry was sent, who threw him a gold coin, which he caught to the cheers of the crowd.

On the day the Goodwood Cup was run, a tipster on the course was telling a large audience that he had a certain winner of the cup at a long price, and if it had not been for an unfortunate accident, he would have been riding in it himself. The man had a terrible squint, which gave him a villainous look. At this point another tipster, immaculate in top hat and morning coat, started to harangue the crowd, his ring adjoining the man with the squint. It was not long before people began to drift from the first ring to the second. Seeing this, the other tipster was provoked into saying, "Ladies and gentlemen, top hats don't find winners. I suppose you know he is, an American quack doctor, over here selling pills."

This was too much for the top-hatted gentleman, who shouted back, "I wish I was, old man! The first thing I should do would be to come over and put that crooked eye straight for you!"

The appearance of Tod Sloan at Goodwood caused a great deal of excitement, as it was the first year an American jockey had ridden over here. He was greeted by the Sussex crowd with laughter and loud cheers. The cheers could be heard in the distance as he cantered to the starting post with the old-timers, Cannon, Loates and others. He rode with a more pronounced crouch than any riding to-day. He did not take long to become a public idol, as he was elsewhere. It is just possible that there is still someone living to-day who saw the great Fred Archer ride at Goodwood. He died 70 years ago.

Few people realise that the Ham Stakes are named in memory of that great sportsman Squire Gratwick, who lived at Ham Manor, Angmering. He bred and raced two very successful horses named Frederick and Merry Monarch, both of which won the Derby.

First published in the *West Sussex Gazette*, 24 July 1954

In his journal, Graburn gives more details of the cheating and swindling that went on at the races. He tells of one incident, before the First World War, where an angry crowd was searching for a "welcher", that is a bookmaker who had failed to pay out on winning bets. Suddenly the cry went up from a member of the crowd, "there he is!" The accused man was pursued by a furious mob, some of whom succeeded in hitting him as they closed in on him. Finally he "neatly vaulted" over the rails of the race track, right in to the arms of a policeman. But all was not what it seemed. The man was actually a Scotland Yard detective, who was working undercover. He had been recognised by the real villains, who directed the fury of the cheated crowd against the plain-clothes policeman, while they made they get-away with their ill-gotten gains.

The race-track swindlers could be both plausible and persuasive, and even those most determined to resist their charms could succumb. Graburn related the case of a friend, a London doctor, who had come to Sussex with his teenage son to go to the races. Lawrie warned him of the silver-tongued tricksters, and the man passed on the warning to his son, lecturing him on the perils of talking to strangers at the races. Unfortunately the father did not heed his own advice, giving up a five pound note to a stranger, whom he never saw again. "I have never," Graburn wrote in his journal, "seen anyone so annoyed with himself as he was on his return, and he was quite upset for several days."

The "Squire Gratwick" referred to in the article was a well-known figure in Victorian Sussex. His passion for horse-racing led him to buy the stables at Michelgrove, which he turned into a centre for thoroughbreds. Graburn also wrote about later trainers at Michelgrove, including William Goater, who once had a 100-1 winner, and W. Halsey, who rode all his own horses, one year riding in both the National and the Derby. Before the Second World War, F. Wotton rode a Michelgrove horse to victory at the Oaks. The stables closed at the outbreak of war and never subsequently re-opened.

There had once been a great mansion at Michelgrove, which rivalled Arundel Castle for size and splendour. For centuries it was the ancestral home of the Shelley family. This family fell out with the Duke of Norfolk over politics in the eighteenth century, and put up rival candidates to the Duke's at general elections. When the Shelley's overstretched themselves financially by building Castle Goring, they sold Michelgrove to the Walker family of Liverpool. The Walkers fared no better, and they sold to the Duke of Norfolk, who had the great mansion demolished. According to Graburn's journal, there are cottages and barns in both Warningcamp and Poling which are built from the rubble of the great house.

Close to the porch of Burpham church is the grave of Ben Brewster, a native of Burpham and a famous jockey in his time. He died after been thrown from his horse on Perry Hill. The poignant lines on his gravestone suggest he didn't easily give up the fight for life:

> *Great grief and pain I underwent,*
> *Till my blessed Lord he for me sent,*
> *Weep not my wife be satisfied,*
> *We prayed for life but God denied*

Brewster died in 1789, aged 43. His gravestone shows him in full gallop on his horse; originally the memorial was painted, showing the jockey in his racing colours.

THE REV. ROBERT FOSTER OF BURPHAM
A naturalist vicar of the 19th century

It was in September 1845, that the Rev. Robert Foster came to Burpham as curate to Mr. Ross. He stayed as such for five years, and then remained in the village as Vicar for another 48 years. This remarkable man was an authority on many subjects, and a great naturalist and botanist. He was often spoken of as another "White of Selborne." Anything unusual in bird or flower he would take to the village school, and tell the children all about it in an interesting way.

In his younger days Mr. Foster would ride miles to see a rare bird or plant. To give an instance of his keenness and energy, he received a letter one July from friends living at Henfield to say that they had a pair of Golden Orioles nesting in their garden. To communicate was too slow for Mr. Foster, so he rose at dawn, and rode on horseback to Henfield, arriving at his friend's house for breakfast. He stayed all day watching the Golden Orioles, and then rode home in the evening. Borrer, the naturalist and a friend of Mr. Foster, is quoted in "Highways and Byways Of Sussex" as having seen 14 of these rare birds in one bush on Henfield Common. This must have been the same year as Mr. Foster's visit, as no such numbers have been seen since.

Mr. Foster was a great "raconteur", and had a store of stories of village life, some amusing and some sad, but all true of the lives and people in this part of Sussex. An old farm-hand, employed in hedge cutting, stopped Mr. Foster soon after his arrival in the village, and asked him if he had been to see part of his flock at Coombe, Lee Farm. The parson replied that he did not know the cottages were in his parish. On being assured that they were, he took directions from the old man, who told him to climb the Leper's Path, and follow the track over the downs which would take him to the cottages. A few days later, Mr. Foster set out, and on reaching the top of the Leper's Path, failed to find the track over the downs, and wandered about for a long time, hoping to see someone from whom he might ask the way. Hearing some sheep bells in the distance, he made for them, and looking over the brow of the next hill, he saw some sheep grazing, watched over by a boy with a dog.

He went to the boy and sat down beside him, glad to rest for a while. After a brief greeting, the boy relapsed into silence, his eyes on the grazing sheep. Then, thinking it was time he went on his way, he turned to the lad and asked him the way to Lee Farm. This the boy told him, adding, "Where be you from, Sir?"

"From Burpham. I'm the new parson and I have come to show the people there the way to heaven."

The boy looked at him in a puzzled way for a few moments, then said, "You be a pretty one to show 'em the way to anywhere, when you don't know the way to Lee Farm yet!"

The village of Burpham was very isolated in those days, before the new road was cut in 1883. The old road wandered up and down hill eventually coming out on to the Worthing road. In spite of this isolation, many celebrities stayed with Mr. Foster. Ruskin, the writer, paid frequent visits, and was often seen of a summer evening sitting on one of the seats overlooking the Arun Valley and Arundel Castle. These seats, which were put up by Mr. Foster, still remain.

Another visitor to Burpham in the early eighties, who later became a famous man, was Cecil Rhodes. He stayed as the guest of Mr. Drewitt (who afterwards became a well known doctor), with several other undergraduate friends, to play cricket against Burpham village. Mr. Foster, who was sitting on the lawn after the match, chatting to the students, turned to Cecil Rhodes and asked him what he was going to do when he left Oxford.

"Oh I shall go out to Africa and knock around for a bit," he replied, a remark which caused much amusement. It will be remembered that many years later, when Queen Victoria asked him what he was doing in South Africa, Rhodes replied, "Extending your dominions, your Majesty."

In the winter of 1898 Mr. Foster, now nearing the end of his long life, went away for what was to be his last holiday. On his return he went, as was his custom, to the village reading room, and told some of the old men sitting there that he had seen a horseless carriage. He added, "I believe some of these young ones will see their bread, beef and beer brought here in such things someday."

He loved old sayings and proverbs, and often used them in the pulpit. Walking through the village one day with a visitor, they met a village girl whom he greeted thus: "Well, my dear, I'm going to marry you on Saturday, aren't I? It seems no time since I married your parents. And where are you going to live?"

"Along with my young man's mother," she replied.

"Your father keeps bees, doesn't he?" said the old man, frowning. "Hasn't he told you that you can't have two queen bees in one hive?"

The last story he told concerned himself. Most of the villagers had succumbed to a serious epidemic of influenza. The church and school were closed and Mr. Foster himself was very ill and unable to visit his parishioners for some weeks. When he had recovered, he was soon going round the cottages, doing what he could. At one cottage occupied by an old man (older than the Vicar), known to all as "Old Shep", he was greeted by the old man, who after upbraiding him for his absence added, "Call yourself the shepherd of the flock; why you ain't fit to look after the tegs!" Tegs, by the way, were the young sheep which had not yet had lambs, and were usually looked after by a shepherd boy.

Old Shep did not live long after this visit, and Mr. Foster buried him. Dying himself soon after, he too was laid in Burpham churchyard, where he had buried so many others.

There is a large window over the west door in Burpham Church, which was put there in memory of Mr. Foster by his parishoners and friends. Unfortunately his tombstone has worn badly and the inscription on it is now difficult to read; but I think the last line was well chosen, "Well done good and faithful friend."

First published in the *West Sussex Gazette*, June 1955

Mr. Foster was certainly a clergyman to be remembered, but one even more worthy of recollection was to follow. Tickner Edwardes was not only vicar of Burpham from 1927-1935, he was also a chronicler of village life, and a keen observer of natural history. This bee-keeping journalist, turned village parson, came to Burpham in about 1897, and died there on Boxing Day 1944. Graburn wrote of him with affection, as did John Cowper Powys, who became one of his few close Burpham friends:

"*He had already written one or two books when I first met him, and while we lived in the village he wrote several more. In those early days Mr. Edwardes lived in what was called the Red Cottage nearby. Not only used he to compose nature sketches for the London periodicals, but he used to write with professional authority on the subject of bees. He kept bees himself, and being exceptionally skilful with his hands could, if my memory fails me not, make his own hives. It was soon after the War, I think, that he decided to take Holy Orders. At any rate the last time I saw him he was not only a clergyman but had recently been appointed Vicar of Burpham. Mr. Edwardes was a man of meticulous nicety in his literary art. I recollect being confounded by the elaborate craftsmanship with which he laboured; pondering on words, taking words up, as it were, and laying them down, just as he did with the materials of his hives. May his ministerial utterances, under that ancient Norman arch, carved in chalk at the top of the little aisle, be as full of the sweetness of the Word as his carefully constructed hives were full of honey! I always liked Mr. Edwardes uncommonly well. I liked the tough-wood texture of his bodily-presence!"*[25]

It would be a shame not to include in this book some extracts of Tickner Edwardes' writing, for he surely deserves to be re-discovered by the book-reading public, and especially by those with an interest in and appreciation of the Sussex countryside and its people. Edwardes was capable of being descriptive and informative, in a straight-forward way, but he could also rise to great heights of literary pathos, and draw the reader into a world that was spiritual as well as merely factual.

Let two examples suffice to prove the point. The first comes from Edwardes' last book, A Downland Year, *published in 1939, the year before Lawrie Graburn began to write down his own stories and recollections. It shows how even in those days, well within the memory of older residents, Burpham and its people were still living a life, that to us appears primitive:*

"They are threshing oats in the rick-yard on the wind-wild morning, and across the yard there is a great careering drift of something that, from a little distance, looks like smoke. It is the dust and finer particles of the chaff that the wind carries farthest. Much of this does not settle in the yard at all, but goes soaring up over the barn-roof and across the meadows in a long cloud-streamer that the sun riddles through and through with gold. The lighter husks, the 'fliers', as the countryfolk call them, are gathering in a pale yellow drift under the rick-yard wall; and there an old woman is busy stuffing armfuls of them into a bed-case of snow-white linen. She will trundle it home presently on the ancient perambulator that stands by, and it will serve her for bed until oat-threshing time comes round again. A chaff-bed is, in point of fact, as softly comfortable as any bed of feathers, only it must be filled with genuine wind-winnowed oat-fliers and changed at every fall."[26]

It is interesting that Tickner Edwardes says "fall", a term we associate nowadays with the United States, rather than "autumn". Many old country words were taken to the "New World" by emigrants, and have entered into everyday usage over there; while in this country, the rural communities, particularly in the south of England have disappeared, and with them their old forms of speech. "Standard English" actually owes more to its Anglo-Norman origins than to the "Old English" dialects of the peasantry. A Sussex rural labourer of a century ago would "reckon" and "guess" about things in a manner worthy of any 'ole Yankee.

The second quote comes from An Idler in the Wilds, *published in 1906; it captures the sense of decay, prevalent in late autumn, but also the promise there is of new things to come:*

"For every leaf that falls a new one is already in the making. The hillside copse of hazel, stripped of its last leaves now, is purple with its promise for next year's greenery. Already the chestnuts have a myriad sappy buds that glisten in the sunshine as the wind rocks their bare branches to and fro. Nothing pauses, nothing looks backwards, everything changes - all but the river. Through all the swift race of growth and leaf and flower, through full maturity and red decline and russet death, until underfoot the dry leaves crackle once more and the only music is the whistling of the empty branches, the river keeps on its eternal way, the one immutable things in a world that is change upon change for ever."[27]

What today is the Burpham House Hotel was once the vicarage, Tickner Edwardes being the last cleric to reside there. Graburn knew its history, and the strange stories surrounding its original occupants, the Gobles, which formed the basis of the following article.

MADAM GOBLE WALKS

In the early part of the last century a girl completely disappeared from the village of Burpham, and though every effort was made to trace her, no clue was ever found.

The girl was French and lived at the Manor House owned by Squire Goble and was governess to his three little daughters. The Squire had a house at Chichester, which he used in the summer, coming to Burpham for the hunting season, and kept his own pack of foxhounds there. The remains of the wall of the kennels can still be seen and large elm trees nearby, blown down about 50 years ago, contained large iron spikes where pieces of horse meat were hung to feed the pack. The trees were known as the Rookery.

Madam Goble was fond of the attractive French girl and conversed with her in French. One September evening, soon after their return to Burpham for the hunting season, the girl said, "The children are all asleep, madam. May I go for a walk?"

"Certainly," was the reply. Late that evening, when she had not returned, a search was made. Two people had met her walking towards the Downs, but after that she was never seen again.

One cannot rule out the possibility that the Arun had claimed another victim, as there had been many drowning accidents at this time near Burpham, the worst being when seven Arundel men from one boat were drowned. There are seven fir trees planted just outside the churchyard in their memory.

The mystery of the girl who disappeared was just before the arrival of Mr. Foster as Vicar in 1845, but he does allude to it in his notes. In the thatched cottage adjoining the house where the girl walked out on that fateful night lived a family; the wife was born in the house, reared 14 children there, and lived to be a great age. Every September she used to say, "Madam Goble walks," but would never say more, or why.

The squire seemed able to do what he liked, with no one to reprimand him. On occasions he had dinner parties for men guests. When they left in the small hours on horseback, the squire would see them off and blow his hunting horn and holloa. This would rouse the pack nearby, and the whole village, too. The noise was "enough to waken the dead," said the old Vicar.

Soon after the squire sold the house and land to the church for a vicarage, and Mr. Foster was the first Vicar to use it. In 1937 it was sold again and a small vicarage built. It is now a guest-house, but still they do say, "Madam Goble walks".

First published in the *West Sussex Gazette*, 24 October 1963

There were a great number of ghost stories and superstitions in the past. It may well have been the long winter evenings without the distraction of radio or television that led to groups of old men conversing over a pint in the village inn. From such conversations surely came many a "tall tale". Graburn gathered much of his information about old country ways from the reminiscences of such men, but he could also back up their recollections with evidence from other sources, such as entries in old diaries or extracts from old newspapers. The following articles all share the common theme of change, and of a way of doing things quite different from that of our own times.

A great social occasion. The hunt assembles outside the George & Dragon. The telegraph pole and motor-cars demonstrate the arrival of modern ways into a once remote rural community.

Reproduced courtesy of West Sussex Library Service.

Huntsmen at Burpham in the 1930s, Lawrence Graburn
is on the left (with hat and pipe).
Reproduced courtesy of West Sussex Library Service.

Huntsmen and hounds at Burpham – 1930s.

Archibald Hey Shorther, 1941, "Whipper-in" to the Hunt, with gruesome trophies. Note the horn placed on top of fence.

Ready for a "Shoot", 1911.

Lawrie Graburn overseeing ploughing at Wepham Farm c. 1930.

Hay-making at Wepham Farm between the wars.
Reproduced courtesy of West Sussex Library Service.

Ploughing with oxen at Alfriston in 1879. Horses had displaced oxen at Wepham a generation earlier, despite the indignant protests of local ploughmen who didn't believe horses were up to the job.

Bygone harvest scene at Wepham.

Hay-stacks at Peppering Farm c.1930.
Reproduced courtesy of West Sussex Library Service.

Hay-stacks at Peppering. The small wooden stucture on wheels is a hen-coop.
Reproduced courtesy of West Sussex Library Service.

The road to Burpham, probably in the 1920s – in the age of the motor-car,
but before the surface was metalled.
Reproduced courtesy of West Sussex Library Service.

Winter scene at Wepham – early twentieth century, close to Wepham House.

George Field the "horse-doctor", with his grandson, also George in 1938. The Field family have been tenants at Splash Farm for over three hundred years.

Reproduced by kind permission of George Field of Splash Farm, Burpham.

VILLAGE BATTLES OF LONG AGO
A feud that lasted for years

If the stories told by young men at the beginning of this century were true - and we have no reason to doubt them - fights between young men in adjoining villages were a common occurrence.

Certain villages seemed to have a permanent grudge against one another, and people can remember football matches 50 years ago between Arundel and Wick when ill-feeling crept in and fights took place. Old people recalled stories of Arundel men returning from Littlehampton on foot at a late hour being waylaid by Wick men and a fight taking place in the main street. A historian at the time said it was a relic of the days when men went to the shore from inland "to help repel the invaders". But it was not only the coast towns which were involved in these fights, and it is difficult to see why they began.

There was one particularly fierce battle between a number of young Arundelians and some Burpham lads on a Sunday evening last century. The old man who told the story and saw the fight as a boy had an elder brother taking part in this battle for Burpham. The fight took place in Burpham before the new road was opened and people walked to the village by the river, climbing the steps sometimes called Jacob's Ladder. Down these steps the running battle continued to the banks of the river, where it ended, both sides being exhausted. There was a lot of blood and one Burpham man had a crooked nose for the rest of his life through a fracture sustained in the fight. The cause of the battle was never known - at any rate, it is not known now.

Other villages had desperate fights and a feud between Amberley men and Cootham and district went on for years. Storrington Fair was the great night. Amberley were well served by a family named Ruff who, it is said, came from the New Forest about 400 years ago when in trouble for killing deer there. The name Ruff has been a household word in Amberley and district ever since, and one of the fighters of 80 years ago used to say, on arrival at Storrington Fair, "Here we are again: Ruff by name, and rough by nature, and we can hold our own with the best." And it was generally agreed that they could, as they were all fine men. Ruffs, Hooks, and Wakehams are still to be found in the district, descendants of the men who fought such battles in the past.

It would be interesting to know the cause of feuds like those which made men of Amberley, now resting in the churchyard, always ready for a fight with the men of Cootham.

First published in the *West Sussex Gazette*, September, 1963

Graburn refers to violence "fifty years ago" at a football match between Wick and Arundel, that would have been in 1913. A report in a local newspaper for May of that year tells of "disgraceful scenes"[28] at a football match at Littlehampton, which led to court proceedings. How wrong we would be to imagine that violence at football matches is something new!

The fights that took place between the young men of different villages appear to have been fairly general at one time, and as the article suggests, they often took place at fairs. A letter written to the West Sussex Gazette *by an elderly reader* recalled the days, before the First World War, when pitched battles took place on the borders of Kent and Sussex, that lasted a whole weekend. The correspondent, who was brought up in the eastern part of the county, concluded by stating that in his youth, "the men of Kent", were regarded as "foreigners", "much as Frenchmen and Germans were".[29] Here perhaps lies the explanation for these fights: they were territorial. Burpham and Arundel were divided by the river, as were Amberley and Cootham. When the territory in question was a county, the passion became that much greater. The Rev. William Parish, in his Dictionary of Sussex Dialect, made the point that anyone from outside Sussex was regarded as a "furriner",[30] or foreigner: this was no idle jest.

Graburn's mention of the Ruff family is interesting. A Samuel Ruff was a notorious smuggler, who died at Clapham in the 1860's. Forty years earlier he had been involved in a vicious skirmish with the coastguards at Littlehampton, during which an officer's sabre had all but cut his nose away. Ruff escaped from the battle, and his wound was bandaged up; however it never properly healed, leaving him with a great ridge across his crooked nose that made him appear like a rhinoceros. Such men became role models for the younger generation.

If brawling at fairs and football matches were the chosen "sports" of the labouring classes, their social superiors sought relief in hunting. The annual slaughter of wildlife was quite extraordinary. In his journal, Graburn describes hundreds of birds, rabbits, and hares being shot in a single day's shooting. But it was hunting with hounds that really made the sap of a country gentleman rise. Today hunting is very controversial, and moves are afoot to outlaw it, yet it in former days it galvinised whole communities.

As mentioned in the "Madam Goble" article, huntsmen could be noisy and unruly, particularly when it came to the "holloa", the dead-raising cry that huntsmen would bawl out when their quarry was sighted. A countryman, working in the fields, might also raise a holloa, if he saw a fox, in the hope of a reward from the huntsman. The article that follows relates one such instance.

GAWD! CAN'T HE 'OLLER!

The following conversation, or something like it, took place in a Sussex inn in the year 1909. Three old labourers were talking about the hunt which had taken place in the neighbourhood that day.

"Did you see the 'ounds to-day, Will?"

"No, I never see 'em, but I 'eard 'em and when I 'eard that 'oller I knowed old Joe Toosley had seen the fox. He was dung spreadun' down Long Acre. Gawd can't he 'oller! I thought he would have been in here before now to tell us about it. I couldn't make nothun' of that 'unt. Our lot don't 'unt Wednesdays and that 'untsman blowed the 'orn and 'ollered different to old George."

Just then Joe came in.

"Come on Joe. We want to hear you. We 'eard you this morning." said his old mate.

"Glad you 'eard me," said Joe. "Well, I kept hearun' the 'orn and 'ounds in the woods and presnsly the fox came out close to me, and the 'untsman came gallopun' up to me. I see he was a fresh one. He told me they had a long run out of their country and wanted to know where he had gone. I told him and that's all I see of the 'unt."

"Then I 'as a bit of luck. A young toff got in the big ditch and asked me if I could get a rope and someone to pull 'un out. I went up to the farm and got a waggon rope and another chap and pulled 'un round and he blundered out 'isself, and I got 5s. for that; that was better than spreadun' two acres of dung."

"You missed the best part of the 'unt Joe," said his old mate. "I didn't know much about 'em till I see two red jacketers galloping across the parson's medder. The fox got into the churchyard and they nearly had 'un under that old yew tree with branches on the ground. He then ran through the school playground just when the boys was coming out. They made a tidy row I can tell you. The fox then went across the field where my governor's old hunter mare and her foal were. Well, that fence was good enough to 'old 'em all the summer, but gallopin' 'orses and the 'orn made the old mare jump the fence and her foal after her. Some say it's cruelty to make 'orses jump ditches, but if they could see that 20-year-old mare and her foal going across country, they would change their story. I had to go four miles to bring them home. Some of the followers had put them in a yard. The old mare was so excited I could 'ardly 'old her."

The hunt ended by the fox going to ground in the hanger. Some surprise was shown when the huntsman immediately called off, and old Joe explained to his mates that a fox was never dug out on another hunt's land, even if he could be poked out with a stick.

The third old man said, "I mind the day when our governor sent us all to the point-to-point and our young governor won the Farmers' Race on that old mare. I see her come here when she was bought out of a drove of Irish colts, and I mind another thing, seeing her well ahead and hearing old Joe Toosley 'oller. Gawd, can't he 'oller!"

First published in the *West Sussex Gazette*, February 1965

By the time that Graburn was writing his articles, in the 1950's, the holloa had disappeared from the hunting spectacle, and even the blowing of horns was being suppressed by more decorous MFH's (Masters of Fox Hounds), who felt that the blowing of whistles was sufficient to alert the rest of the hunt that a fox had been sighted. Graburn wrote of another old "hollerer" in an article published in 1952:

One MFH of the past liked to hear a rousing view holloa and often sent a yeoman farmer forward for a view, in a large wood noted for its echo; that farmer had a wonderful holloa. On one occasion the Master, heading the field, had nearly reached the spot where the farmer stood - thinking the wood was blank - when the fox broke covert. The resultant holloa was so great that four horses bolted, two into the hazel undergrowth, dislodging their riders. This little episode would certainly not have happened if he had only blown a whistle.

Graburn also noted that the village children mimicked the hunt in their games: "A favourite game with the village lads was called 'foxhunting' and was played at night round the village and on the Downs. Two went as foxes and had to keep together and shout every few minutes, so that the pack could follow. If the pack got close and the foxes did not shout to let them know where they were, the pack would all chant together "'oller, 'oller, or else puppy dogs won't foller'."

Rural labourers were never well paid. In one of his articles, Graburn described the various means by which a poor man could improve his earnings:

An old man who died not so long ago described to us his Christmas as a boy in the last century. He left school at the age of 11 and was unable to get a job on the farm with the horses, so he had to go to another farm two miles away and tend sheep for 3s. 6d a week. He was the eldest of seven children, he told us, and he often had to go off in the morning with the top of a cottage loaf with no butter or cheese, and if he could, crawl through a hedge and get a turnip or a swede.... His father received 14s. a week, but for that he also had to feed the bullocks on Sundays.

We asked what presents the children had, and he said, "All the same, a penny and an orange each." Once while tending the flock on Boxing Day, he heard the hounds and horn and the fox came past him and all the hounds. And then a lot of "red jacketers" came along and asked him to open a gate which was chained up; this he did and two of them gave him 1s. each. And then a hare jumped up in the middle of the pack and they got hold of her, but the huntsman whipped them off and gave her to our friend and told him to take her home.

"My old dad was a wonderful chap at picking up a shilling or two to help out with the food," he said. "One day there was a terrible fog on the hill and some of the children heard shouts of 'Lost, lost!' on the hill. They found dad in the wood-house and told him, and he found two ladies and two gentlemen lost. They said they would never have got home. They gave dad 5s. and were very pleased to get home."

The old man always said, "None of us got very big because we never got enough food. They didn't blow 'em up at school with milk every day like they do now." But in spite of that, he turned out a remarkable man. He recorded one more story of his old father. He used to go to Arundel most Saturday nights, and usually waited till later in the evening, when Dick Reed the butcher would step out on the pavement and holloa with a loud voice, "Wild rabbit and a pound of pork a shilling!" He always had a shilling's worth in the winter time. It was only in ways like that the labourers could make the money go round."[31]

CHANGES IN VILLAGE LIFE
Days when amusements were few and simple

I have been looking at two old diaries kept in this village during the last century, both showing what a simple life was led by the village people of those days. One was kept by the Vicar from 1845 to 1899 and the other by a lady for a shorter period at the end of the century.

The Vicar records burying old people who had lived their whole lives in the village and never been more than ten miles from it. Amusements were very scarce, so the young men collected in the blacksmith's shop in the winter evenings after the day's work, chiefly for light and warmth. Others went sparrow catching with nets and caught large numbers.

The lady diarist records that when anything did occur, it was hailed with delight - even a course of lectures through Lent on gardening arranged by the Vicar. This was so popular that the hall was too small to hold all who wanted to attend. An old shepherd who came a little late to the first lecture was told at the door that the place was full. He was heard to say, "I wants to get inside there somewhere, they say this man can tell us how to grow a gallon of taters to a root."

When two ladies took a house in the village they were determined to make the winter evenings brighter for the young people. The first thing they did was to engage a conjuror. Few had ever seen one, and they were amazed at what he did and talked of it for weeks. The titbit was when he pulled a rabbit out of an old carter's inside coat pocket, and said, "You've got an old poacher over there!"

The ladies were delighted at the pleasure they had given, and after a children's party at Christmas, which was the best ever seen in the village, it was arranged to have a party for elderly people in the new year. This was a great treat to the old people, as the ladies arranged for games with prizes to take place after a meal.

The Vicar, walking round before the games, stopped at a table occupied by three old women and caused laughter when he said:

Put three old women round three cups of tea,
And they'll talk of more scandal than you'll commonly see.
But put three old men round three gallons of beer,
And they'll talk of more work than they'll do in ten year.

The lady diarist records a story at this time which is still remembered by a few old people and which had a happy ending. A young man, the son of the wheelwright and undertaker, became very ill with pleurisy. He was very popular, and a great favourite in the village. The old doctor being ill, a locum was sent to see him. This did not please the villagers as he looked so young, and they very quickly called him the "boy doctor".

Every day he was driven to see his patient by the old groom in a high dog-cart. One day he was seen leaving the village at a great pace after visiting the young man. Bad reports were heard, but he was back at the house in half an hour. This was the end, the villagers said, when the heard the "boy doctor" had cut poor George about, and hope was nearly given up.

On the following Sunday the diarist and her two children, passing the house of the young man on the way to church, saw his father leaning over his gate mopping his pox-marked face with a large red handkerchief. The lady said, "I am afraid to ask after poor George, as his father is crying and I think the end has come." However, she asked if there was any change in poor George, and never did she have such a surprise as when his father said, "George, he's ever so much better, settun up in bed and eatun enough sloppy stuff to keep a pack of foxhounds."

George made a full recovery and lived 60 years in the village after that, and the "boy doctor's" reputation went up by leaps and bounds.

The greatest change of this century was the arrival of the main water. Until then every pint had to be wound up from a deep well every day of the year, often by a worker after a long day's toil. Electric light was viewed with suspicion at first. Only 21 years ago, one old resident when asked if he was going to have it, said, "I ain't doing to 'ave any of that tackle in the 'ouse. It might blow the bloomin' place up."

The third big change was the passing of the horse. Until 50 years ago, our village had 80 to 100 horses, including cart horses, colts, riding and driving horses. Now we have one blacksmith and not a single horse of any kind.

First published in the *West Sussex Gazette*, 13 December 1959

It is rather surprising that the wheelwright could afford to pay for a doctor to visit his son every day, but it may have been that one of the gentlemen of the village covered the costs. Generally speaking, poor people in those days relied on herbal remedies and superstitious cures, as these were free. These days the doctor is free, while the herbal cures are purchased at the cost of several pounds from health food shops!

SHUTTLES POND, BURPHAM

How long this wonderful spring has served mankind, no one can say. Here a very old disused sunken road wends its way down to it from the Downs. This road is called "The Stopples", and along it ancient Britons came to fill their skin water-carriers. They also brought their cattle to drink at the spring when their ponds on the hills were dry. The fields each side are still known as the "Pens" and "Shuttles". Here the water from the "Pens" drove the mill mentioned in Domesday Book. This water-mill ground the corn for the village and district.

The pond is tidal, and when it is low-tide the water runs underground, and can be seen discharging into the river Arun, but at high-tide it cannot run out, as the weight of water in the river holds it back; it then runs over the road to a deep ditch, and so into the Arun that way. This has been a source of trouble to motorists and others, who may come to Burpham in the morning and find a pefectly dry road. On their return, a few hours later, they are astonished to find water rushing across the road, three feet deep. Many water-logged cars have been pulled out at different times. Luckily there are two ways into Burpham, so that motorists, finding their exit blocked, can leave by the other road.

This fine spring was tapped about twenty years ago, nearly a mile north of the pond, where an inexhaustible supply of pure water was found, which now supplies Littlehampton and district. Another bore-hole has recently been made on the same site, with a view to helping Worthing in the future.

A picture, over fifty years old, has just been found. Two of the men are wearing "yorks", a strap below the knee - now never seen. A farm-worker at that time was only partly dressed without them. Just beyond the low hovel in the picture us a fine old timbered house, where, in the past, the Court leet was held. This was presided over by three or four of the elders of the village, who dealt with minor offences, and settled disputes and village affairs. The cottage is now owned by Mr. O'Neil, whose ancestors came from Ireland to Burpham in 1861 to help with the harvest. They liked it so much that they never returned to the Emerald Isle.

The stream over the road is the boundary between the hamlet of Wepham and the village of Burpham.

First published in the Sussex County Magazine, December 1954

The bore-holes referred to in the article have, over the years, had the effect of reducing the frequency with which the "splash" has flooded over the road: equally the pond has diminished in size. However, the exceptionally wet autumn of 2000 resulted in water several feet deep flooding across the road, as the little stream rose to unprecedented heights.

The son of the Mr. O'Neil mentioned in the article still lives in the village, in a house only a short distance from the old Court Leet cottage, where his parents lived for many years.

Lawrie Graburn was first and foremost a countryman, who spent his working life farming. Most of the early notes in his journal concern wildlife and natural history. It is a selection of this type of article that appears on the following pages.

MARCH HARES
Extraordinary capers in the mating season

Most people have heard the saying "mad as a March Hare", which like all old proverbs is founded on fact, as at this time of year hares seem to behave in the most peculiar way. When in a hare country I have seen 20 or more in a lump, some standing on their hind legs facing each other like boxers sparring, and others jumping and bounding about and cutting the most extraordinary capers. All this occurs during the mating season, when the males are fighting. At other times they are timid, shy animals.

Rabbits and hares are often spoken of as if they were alike, when in reality they are different in every way. For instance, a rabbit is born underground naked and blind. The hare is born above ground, covered with fur, and its beautiful golden eyes open. Hares have three or four families during the summer, usually two, three, or four at a time. They are born in a field, and after two days will not be found together, nor will the mother be with them. The young will be several yards apart, and the mother in another field. This is nature's way of protection, so that if an enemy finds one, it does not get the whole family.

I have only known one man who has seen a hare visit her young, He was looking over a hedge into a large grass field, when he saw a hare coming straight towards him at a slow pace. He kept very still, and when she got within a few yards of him she ran round him in circles making grunting noises. Immediately three little leverets ran to her and sucked as she stood there. In a few minutes she left and the leverets disappeared in the grass. I am sure a naturalist with a camera would have liked to have been there. The period of gestation is a month, whence the old saying "A hare and a mare go a year", the mare going 11 months.

A hare relies on its pace and cunning to escape from its enemies. A hare hunted by harriers or beagles, when tired, will turn a fresh one out of its seat and take its place, and let the hounds go full cry after the new one. They sometimes sit very tight in their seat or form. They have several scratches made, and a change of wind will find them in a fresh place. Shepherds and other countrymen can often kill one before she rises from her seat by making a trusty dog sit, or by putting a coat on a stick a few yards away. The hare will watch the dog or coat, while the man makes a slight detour and kills it with a sharp blow from behind. A hare's eyes are set up so that it can see a dog which is pursuing it and turn sharply to get away, but it will run right up to a person standing still in a road in front of it.

In the days when everyone believed in witchcraft, old women if they were ugly and eccentric were thought to be able to turn themselves into these animals and vice versa. If a hare was seen near their home, it was enough for them to be blamed for some trivial mishap such as a horse going lame, milk turning sour or hens not laying, and they were dragged off and burned as witches. It seems strange to us nowadays that this shy and harmless animal should have been connected with witchcraft. Even now in some parts of the country such as Cornwall the superstition still lingers.

First published in the *West Sussex Gazette*, 8 March 1956

Hunting hares with hounds was already a memory by 1956, but one which was warmly recalled by the West Sussex Gazette's *older readers. One correspondent remembered the large number of hare-hunts, or "harriers", that existed in Sussex before the First World War:*

"The South Coast Harriers [were] kennelled at Hope Cottage, Patching, and these were also listed as stag-hounds. There were also the Iping Harriers of Mr. Hamilton of Iping, the Storrington Beagles were kept by Mr. Faithfull's students, whose country was later hunted by that great hare hunter, Mr. Ewen Goff. Mr. Guy Paget kept the Shopwyke Beagles at Shopwyke House, Chichester; Mr. Leslie Constable a pack at Ifold; and May St. John a pack of harriers at Slinfold. Doubtless there were others, but I am sure reminiscences of any of these old packs, and the sport they showed would give pleasure to many of your readers to-day." [30]

The letter was signed *"Harehunter", and stimulated a correspondence over the next few weeks. It does indeed seem strange in these days that the hunting of the "shy and harmless" hare should have been so fondly remembered, but nostalgia is a powerful emotion! One correspondent declared, "What happy memories 'harehunter's' letter recalls", while another remembered a time when the Leigh Park Beagles were taken by train to hunt a hare at Selsey. The letter described how the artful hare evaded his pursuers by swimming out to sea, where the hunt could not follow. Eventually the huntsmen gave up the chase and boarded the train for the return journey to Havant, before realising that one of the dogs was missing. The lost hound made its own way back to the kennels, walking through the night - a distance of sixteen miles. "Not bad. Those were the days," concluded the wistful correspondent.*

By the time of the 1956 article, *hares were mostly being killed by shooting. In the last entry in his journal, for February 1965, Graburn recorded that in just three days "there have been record hare shoots". In one day 333 were killed at Wepham and Lee farms, with 240 being shot at Peppering and North Stoke, and 400 at Wiston. This made a total of 1,000 hares killed in the space of three days. The brown hare, unlike the rabbit, which was introduced by the Normans, is a native animal. Since the 1970's hares have adapted themselves to new habitats, occupying the margins of woodlands, as well as downland and common, where they were traditionally found.*

Graburn *also mentioned the connection between hares and witchcraft. In actual fact witches were not burned in England, but hanged. It is interesting to note that Sussex condemned fewer witches to death than any other county in England. Only four such sentences were handed down, and all of those were in the wealden, as opposed to the downland, district of the county. This raises the question as to whether belief in witchcraft was weaker in Sussex than elsewhere, or whether the local Justices simply refused to take it seriously. The last explanation seems to be the most likely, for there is plenty of evidence to suggest that the country people believed in witchcraft. Mrs. Charlotte Latham, in her little book on West Sussex superstitions, written in 1868, gave many instances of these beliefs, as did the Sussex antiquarian, M. A. Lower, writing at about the same time. What is more surprising is to find evidence from the twentieth century. The following item, which appeared in* Sussex Notes and Queries *in 1933, shows how inseparable the hare and the witch still were in the minds of the older rural folk:*

"An instance of the survival of a belief in witch-craft comes from West Sussex. An old man, well over 80, hearing witch-craft described as 'All rubbish', got very excited and exclaimed 'All rubbish! it aint. Why, I knew a witch myself in this very village. Her daughter's still alive. I'll tell you what happened once' He told of the bewitching of animals, and mostly of Farmer ------'s horse, which was 'overlooked' by the witch so that it became quite helpless. 'Why, it couldn't even die. They got a gun and shot it through the head, but even then it could not die. It did not die until they got her to let it die. She only

wanted to do Master ---- harm and she was satisfied when she had given him all that trouble. She had a book of charms we all know and she used it. But one of her daughters took it out of the village - and a good thing, too! We don't want any truck with that sort of thing.' In answer to the question as to his own personal experiences of the witch, the old man told how he went to fetch help for a sick person very late at night. 'By that hedge over there I saw the dark form of a woman. On getting up to her I saw it was Mrs ----. I says, "Why, Mrs. ----, you aint no call to be out so late as this!" And instead of her I saw a hare running through a gap in the hedge. I shall never forget it, not to my dying day.'

"The old man, telling his story so excitedly, sitting bolt upright in his armchair by the kitchen fire, had never been more than a day's walk from his own village and knew nothing of the book lore which records the belief all over Europe that a witch trying to escape from men turns herself into a hare."[51]

Graburn wrote of his own encounter with an old countryman, who told a tale of the supernatural concerning hares and witches. His story is similar to others recorded by folklorists across England, although it has some original touches. What really marks it out however is the date – 1954 - which is certainly very late for the survival of such a story, and shows how remote and isolated the downland communities in that part of Sussex once were:

I recently visited a man nearly 90 years old, and he told me this little "hare" story. His father lived on the edge of a large wood, and had four sons, of whom this old man was the youngest. They were named Matthew, Mark, Luke, and John. One end of their thatched cottage was occupied by an old woman, who was held in awe by the boys. Most days their father was away from home working for the squire in the big woods. When the boys were troublesome, their mother used to threaten to take them into the old woman next door.

The squire lived nearby, and it was his custom to invite the local Harriers to meet at his house every season, where they were well entertained. The huntsman, an amateur, was well known for his generosity to the farm workers when hounds were about. Hares being scarce, their father would send word by one of the boys where one could be found. This meant a present of 2s 6d - a sum equal to a hard day's work at this time.

On this occasion he was at the meet himself, and the huntsman seeing him said, "I hope we shall find to-day, as we had a blank day on Wednesday." The reply was, "We've found already, Sir. There she lays on that brow, in the grass field, where she has been a-sitting for several days."

The huntsman rode straight to the spot, and the hare rose in full view of the pack and all the followers. A long hunt followed. Two hours later the four boys were playing in their garden, when they heard the horn, and peeping through the hedge, they saw a tired hare enter the wood. The hounds were not far behind in full cry, but as they reached the wood the scent vanished and all was quiet.

The huntsman asked the boys if they had seen her, and they showed him the spot where she had disappeared in the thick undergrowth. Dismounting, he handed the reins to one of the boys and walked into the wood. After a few minutes, to use the old man's words, "There was an 'ell of a squalkin'." The huntsman's voice and whip were heard, the hounds having attacked the old woman who lived next door, as she was crawling about on her hands and knees, picking up hazel nuts. She limped back to the cottage, with clothes torn and blood running, when the hounds were whipped off.

They never found the hare, but they reckoned she turned into the old witch who squealed just like a hare, when the hounds set on her.

The hare suffered for its intelligence, and was only hunted because of the cunning it displayed in outwitting its pursuers. Equally this shrewdness was seen by many simple folk as evidence of the supernatural, hence the crazy stories about hares really being witches.

HOW SKYLARKS WERE CAUGHT FOR THE TABLE

Many people have noticed and written about the scarcity of Skylarks in parks and fields in towns, where years ago they were common and could be seen in summer soaring in song close to the houses. Why this should be is difficult to explain, and why they were so plentiful when large numbers were netted or shot for the table of gourmets. Until the beginning of this century larks were to be seen hanging in poulterers' shops where they had a ready sale, being considered a great delicacy.

There were two ways of catching larks - netting by night with long silk nets or with the aid of lark glasses on sunny days. The first method does not need much explanation, except to say that two men, several yards apart, would drag the net over a field, thus entangling the larks roosting on the ground. Regarding the second method - how many people know what a "lark-glass" is? How was it used to lure these little birds in such large numbers?

I have a lark-glass in my possession, with which the previous owner on one occasion shot over 300 birds on a sunny January day. The procedure was to put up the glass about two feet high, in a field where larks were feeding in large numbers, and make it revolve by clockwork or by pulling a string. The gunner would be concealed in a hedge at a suitable distance. The larks would flutter over the shining glass, and when they were thick enough, the gunner would shoot, killing a dozen or so at a shot.

People in London made special visits to Brighton and Eastbourne in the winter to feed on these dainty morsels in pies and puddings. This continued for several years after wheatears had ceased to be caught.

Larks squat like a game bird and have a strong scent. They were quite a menace to shooting men, when setters and pointers were almost always used. Often a dog would stand and point, and would not move until someone had flushed the bird squatting a yard or two from its nose. In the days of falconry, sparrow hawks were trained to take larks on the wing. These hawks were considered the most difficult hawk to train, and were called "ladies hawks", I suppose because they were used by "my lady" of the castle or manor when she went out "hawking" over the fields and meadows in mediaeval times.

In the recent cold snap I noticed a flock of larks feeding in a clover field near the Downs. It was difficult to guess the number, but my estimate exceeded 1,000. Many or all of this flock might have come from the continent. Since the cold spell, they are not flocked so closely, but are still to be seen. In an adjoining field of rape and turnips was a flock of several hundred linnets feeding on the charlock seed, which had ripened and fallen to the ground.

First published in the *West Sussex Gazette*, 2 February 1955

THE DISAPPEARANCE OF "THE LITTLE BROWN BIRD"

Mechanical farming drives out the partridges

The general decrease of the partridge or "little brown bird" as it is called by country folk, is a sad blow to sportsmen all over the country. But for the fact that they are such wonderful parents, their numbers would be even less than they are. Of all their enemies, man must be the chief culprit. Wherever he settles, new dwellings spring up over the countryside, and each new house generally has a cat to destroy a sitting bird or young family.

Secondly, modern farming is to blame. Tractors plough so fast that all the stubbles are ploughed in a few weeks after the harvest is gathered, leaving no food on the ground for the partridge when the bad weather comes. And thirdly the spraying of weeds in the corn kills all insect life. A farmer who used to farm a large acreage near the coast pointed out to me where, in the first years of this century he had shot 20 brace of partridges on what was then a turnip field. Now it is a mass of houses and bungalows.

It was said in the past that Southdown sheep and partridges could not thrive without the ploughshare. That old saying has proved right, as since the war they have increased on land that has been ploughed.

Fifty years ago, when partridges were very plentiful, and root crops bad owing to a hot dry summer, there was in consequence no cover for the birds to lie in and they were very wild. So gunners put up a kite in the shape of a large hawk and the birds would lie like stones on the bare ground. I remember when I was a child, one mild January day, watching my father tie such a kite to a hedge, and then with a setter ranging in front of him, walk across a large fallow field. On his return he had shot five brace of French partridges. These had increased in numbers to such an extent that it was thought at the time that they would oust the English partridge.

The extraordinary bravery of a partridge has to be seen to be believe. Nature has given them neither strong beak nor spur to defend themselves or their family. All they can do is to buffet with their wings a crow or magpie, which will endeavour to take the baby chicks, one by one, to feed its hungry family.

If surprised by a dog, the parent birds will run round in circles, acting the broken wing trick, and even allowing a dog to pick them up in its jaws. I saw this happen while walking on the Downs with a friend whose dog, a trained retriever, deposited a partridge unhurt at his master's feet.

The bravest thing I have witnessed, though some countrymen may have seen something to surpass it, occurred on June 12, 1935. Passing over a railway crossing at mid-day in an early heat wave, I noticed that a train had set the dead grass alight on the railway bank. I sat on the gate for a few minutes, watching the little tongues of flame running along the dead grass. Suddenly I became aware of the agitated note of partridges close by, but could not see anything. Jumping off the gate I ran through the smoke and found two birds side by side flapping with their wings at the flames which had reached their nest. With difficulty I stamped out the fire just in time, and on examining the eggs, I found them unnaturally hot. Holding them to my ear, I could hear the chicks squeaking inside. All this time the birds stayed close beside me. They seemed to know I was helping them. I am sure that had there been no fire, they would have turned on the broken wing trick to lure me away. The next day I looked at the nest and found 16 shells - all had hatched. In the adjoining field I walked into the family, who failed to recognise their saviour of the previous day.

What a paradise it would be for the modern sportsman if partridges were as plentiful as they were in the days of Squire Osbaldeston, Master of the Quorn, who lived in the first half of the 19th century. The Squire was continually making large wagers. One of the best known was when he backed himself for 1,000 guineas to ride 200 miles in ten consecutive hours. While training for this event, he shot partridges every day, and made another large bet that he would shoot 100 partridges in a day without assistance. He had two loaders with him, as it was in the days of the muzzle loader guns, when powder and shot had to be rammed down the barrel by hand before firing. Needless to say the Squire won both wagers with time to spare.

First published in the *West Sussex Gazette*, August 1955

The decline of the English partridge has continued. Experts in recent years have written of the introduction of Rock partridges into the county, along with a hybrid known as an "Oridge". Evidently ornithologists have difficulty in telling them apart. The decline of the English, grey, partridge, at the expense of the French, red-legged, partridge is due to the better survival of the latter during harsh winters. Presumably the mild winters of recent years should be to the advantage of the English partridge.

HELL BRAMBLES

A countryman's opinion of the wild rose

Poets and others have written and sung the praises of the wild rose, which in June lightly trails its delicate pinky-white blossoms in festoons across our hedges.

I am afraid Old John, an 86-year-old farm worker, was not an admirer of this hedgerow bush. The beauty of its flowers and its glowing red hips in the autumn meant nothing to him, and he used to say disgustedly, "I calls 'em 'ell brambles, and I 'ates they things."

This name for the wild rose is well known in Sussex, and is used by country folk, though botanists would probably call it by its Latin name, *rosa arvensis*. It is only those who come into contact with this bush while doing their daily work, that dislike it so much. I have seen a copse cutter take infinite care to clear a large wild rose bush, and put it on the fire before cutting the hazel sticks, saying "They've got so many ends to 'em."

Old John used to say, "There's only one thing they're any good for, and when you wants one you can't find it." He went on to explain, "You see Sir, when you're ferreting and you 'as a dead rabbit in a deep 'ole, you wants 'un out. If you be lucky enough to find a long 'ell bramble sucker, you can wind 'un out with it and save yourself a couple of hours 'ard diggin'."

After the following experience with the wild rose, I fully endorse Old John's remarks about "'ell brambles". It was many years ago that I started bee-keeping. I had bought a stock of Italian bees from a well-known apiary, and a new hive ready for the swarm, which I particularly wanted. It was a fine warm June day and my brother and I had changed for an early lunch as we were going for a river picnic in the afternoon. I had put on a new suit for the occasion. Just as we were on the point of leaving, the gardener called to say that the Italian bees had swarmed. Running out, we saw that the bees were not going to settle, and in fact were flying away. My brother raced after them and I, remembering that there was a horse saddled and bridled in the stable, was soon galloping after him. By the time I reached him he was finding it difficult to keep up with the bees, so I took over. All was well until we reached a large wood, where I lost sight of them. So I stopped, and hearing the sound of an axe, I went along the ride. There I came upon a woodman, who told me that he had heard the bees go over, so I knew I had lost them. This annoyed me as I was particularly anxious to get the swarm, but worse was to follow.

Turning my horse's head for home, I stopped to light my pipe before riding down a steep track cut out of the wood. About half way down, the horse reached up and nibbled at a wild rose, pulling it down across my knees. He then walked on and the brambles hanging on to my trousers tore large rents in both legs. I put my pipe in my pocket and got out my knife to cut myself free. Having done this, I got to the bottom and galloped across a large field. Pulling up at the end, I was horrified to find smoke pouring out of my coat. I soon saw that my pocket was burned out, and my pipe gone. I looked sadly at the charred hole in my coat and then at my torn trousers and felt that this was indeed an unlucky day. I had spoilt my new suit and lost my pipe and a good swarm of bees.

Arriving home I changed into an older suit and went to the picnic. I thought it was the limit to be asked, "Why aren't you wearing your new suit?"

So I think I have good reason to say with Old John, "'ell brambles! I 'ates they things."

First published in the *West Sussex Gazette*, 2 February 1956

A less alarming, although equally appropriate name given to the wild rose and the blackberry bush by country folk, was "the lover", for which Graburn had an amusing anecdote concerning a lady, new to the village, who went out walking in the country one day:

She met no-one until she saw old George trimming a hedge. He took one glance at her and said, "I see you've got a lover, mum. He looks like he'll hold 'un tight, too. You've likely to get another before you gets back to the village; I haven't raked up yet." The lady was infuriated. "How dare you speak to me like that my man! I shall tell my husband when I get home."

The misunderstanding was later cleared up, and there was no need for the husband to demand an apology from the misunderstood countryman.

The Rev. Parish, in his dictionary, recorded the following entry from East Sussex: Lawyer - a long bramble full of thorns, so called because, "When once they gets a holt an ye, ye do'a'nt easy get shut of 'em."[32]

GIVE A DOG A BAD NAME AND HANG HIM

Few people know that until well under 100 years ago hanging dogs was the usual way of destroying them. Vets had not arrived to give the injection of to-day. Constant reference is made in old books to the practice. In that near classic, *Parson Woodforde's Diary*, he says, "My best greyhound bitch, 'Flos', went into a neighbour's house and stole a leg of mutton uncooked," and he casually adds, "My man, Ben, did hang her last night."

About the same time there is a description of a very long fox-hunt which started in the morning and went on till dark, when the fox was seen to enter Tortington woods, nr. Arundel. There it was chased by a cur dog. This finished the hunt, but two members secured the varmint and hung him to a bough. These instances show that it was the usual way, and not considered cruel.

People with pets or faithful old friends usually went to someone who undertook the unpleasant execution when the time had come to part. An old man who worked on the land the whole of his life near Arundel told a man in 1864 that he was better off killing dogs at half-a-crown and cats at a shilling than he had been for years. He was leading three dogs from a village; two were old and nearly blind and owned by an old lady who was very distressed at parting with them. The old man tried to cheer her up by saying, "Don't cry about them, Mum; you'll be with them again before long." The third dog was an "extra" as it had killed a lot of poultry in the night, and the owner asked him to take it. The old dog killer told the man he could kill and bury those three dogs and get 7s 6d, but if he went dung spreading it would take him three days to earn that.

It seems that at that time any dog, good or bad, that made a mistake was instantly hanged - if only for killing a chicken. An exception was made 100 years ago. It was the custom of tenant farmers to walk a couple of puppies for the Hunt. Mr. Drewitt, a well-known farmer of North Stoke, who always returned a good couple, had the misfortune to let his escape at night, just before they returned to the kennels, with the terrible result that they found a pen of fat sheep and drove them down the hill into the muddy river, where 28 were drowned. The noble Lord visited the scene of the disaster with his huntsman the next day, and arrangements were made for the culprits to return to kennels, where the huntsman assured his lordship that they were the best bitches he had seen and would soon know the difference between sheep and a fox, the report says.

First published in the *West Sussex Gazette*, 7 September 1961

COUNTRY BELIEFS ABOUT THE MOON AND THE TIDES

The old belief that mushrooms grow best with a waxing moon is still widely held, and there are other country beliefs about the effect of the moon and the tide on the growth of vegetation and the behaviour of animals - even humans. I don't know if the scientists are agreed now that there is really no connection, but 40 years ago it would have been very difficult to convince many an old countryman of this.

An old rabbit catcher, wiring or netting rabbits, said, "Shan't get many to-night; the moon ain't right for them to run far."

But the old mole catcher said, "It ain't no good settin' traps till the end of the week till the tide starts makun'." He was so sure that he took his spade into several gardens where he had been asked to set traps, and threw out several when they were working.

Many old attendants at lunatic asylums were convinced that some patients were worse at some phases of the moon. Many doctors disagreed, but others did not rule it out entirely.

Old shepherds have always been superstitious and even to-day there are good men who think the mating of the flock when the rams are turned out is ruled by the moon. A common saying in the past was, "How's the moon now? We'll turn them out at the end of the week."

But it took an early Brains Trust quiz on the wireless, round about 20 years ago, to cause the heated discussion that went on so long in our village. Most of those who took part have passed on, but there are some left who share their views.

The wording of the question I am not sure of, but it was the answer which upset the old countrymen. The question was roughly, "Do the team agree that the growth of mushrooms is ruled by the moon?" The question-master read it over twice and then Professor Joad said, "Pack of nonsense. Old woman's tale!" No other member of the panel spoke. This reply infuriated several old timers in the village, among them two old shepherds who were hardly civil to anyone next evening in the inn.

"What does he know about it? Stuck up in London all his life! I could tell him there are no mushrooms now, but in a week's time there will be bushels. What would he say to that?"

"Ah", said the other old shepherd. "He thinks he knows all about it. He thinks - but we knows. We aren't up there all day for nothing and don't look for mushrooms till the moon's right. I should like to get him up there for a while. I could show him some things he wouldn't know much about."

"I daresay you could, Jim, but if he got you up in London he could show you a few things that would make you stare about a bit, you know."

First published in the *West Sussex Gazette*, 26 October 1961

Recent studies suggest that the old men in the pub may have known more than the old man on the radio after all. Certainly sleeplessness, anxiety, and more serious forms of mental illness have been observed to increase during the Full Moon.

Writing in 1868, Mrs. Charlotte Latham of Fittleworth noted many superstitious rites connected with the different phases of the moon. Even the course of true love could be affected by the moon:

"Should a girl wish to know what will be the personal appearance of her future husband, she must sit across a gate or stile and look steadfastly at the new moon that rises after New Year's Day. She must go alone, and must not have confided her intention to anyone, and when the moon appears, it is thus apostrophised:

> *All hail to thee, Moon, all hail to thee!*
> *I pray thee, good Moon, reveal to me*
> *This night who my husband must be.*

I know of no recent instance of this charm being tried, but I do hear that the new January moon is still watched by our Sussex maidens.[33]

It is hard not to believe that such a custom had its origins in pre-Christian, Saxon times, when the Moon was truly worshipped. It is striking that such beliefs were "still lingering" in 1868, when in downland villages in particular, the Church played such a dominant role in peoples' lives.

THE CUCKOOS ARE LEAVING

There are more stories and legends told about Cuckoos than about any other bird, especially among countrymen. Now the old birds are leaving us at the end of July, the young ones remaining till September. It is still one of nature's mysteries how the urge comes to leave and when to go.

A lot more has been learnt about this strange bird since the book "The Cuckoo's Secret" was published a few years ago. Experts observed so carefully that they could say within a few hours that a Cuckoo would lay an egg in a certain nest.

But the old countrymen of the past had ideas of their own on some of the Cuckoo's habits, and some are still held to-day. A conversation between an old farm worker and a copse cutter in a pub several years ago shows this.

The copse cutter said he had seen a Cuckoo several times on March 21. "You never seen no Cuckoo, she aint here yet," said the other.

"I knows she be. I see her right enough. My 'pinion be they are 'ere ever so long before they starts 'ollering. My old dad always said they couldn't 'oller till they could find some little birds' eggs to suck, and that ain't fur out neither."

The belief that Cuckoos turned into hawks and stayed the winter is not spoken of now that hawks are rare birds, but it was well believed before migration was understood. Less than 200 years ago nothing was known of migration, and such naturalists as Gilbert White at Selborne searched the caves and holes in the Hanger at Selborne for the swallow family, as that was the last place where they were seen before migration.

I heard a Cuckoo story in the last week in June this year. An old farm hand was digging a garden, and while he was speaking to his employer, a Cuckoo started calling in the nearby wood.

The employer said, "You won't hear much more of that this year, George."

"A good job too, Sir, the dirty beasts spittun' about all over the place. I got covered with their spit comin' through the copse here this morning. You won't see it much longer now they are gone."

First published in the *West Sussex Gazette*, 25 July 1963

There was once a belief that an irascible old woman kept all the cuckoos in her house during the winter, then released them all at Heathfield Fair on 14 April, which was therefore known as "Cuckoo Fair". There was also a rhyme, popular with children, that credited the cuckoo with drying out the land after the rains of winter, but also damned it as the robber of other birds' nests:

> *The Cuckoo is a merry bird, she sings as she flies,*
> *She brings us good tidings and tells us no lies;*
> *She picks up the dirt in the spring of the year,*
> *And sucks little birds' eggs to keep her voice clear.*

THE HELPLESSNESS OF LARGER ANIMALS

Many people who study nature are interested in the way our Maker gave the lower and smaller animals the sense to save their young from danger of different sorts, but does not seem to have given the same gift to the large animals.

Most people have seen cats carrying their kittens and bitches their puppies. In fact all small animals will carry their young when threatened by danger from fire or water, and many brave things have been seen and recorded. But what about horses and cows? A heifer has been known to drive her horns through a dog that approached too near in a field where she was having her calf, but had no sense to move the calf from other danger.

A railway engine driver, who drove a train to London each morning, saw a heifer staring into a dry ditch. The second morning she was still there, and being a countryman, he noticed her extended udder. So at the next station he asked the stationmaster to telephone the farmer. He was just in time, and there was a calf in the ditch and luckily it was saved. Most stock owners have lost calves in this annoying way. If it had been a mouse's nest in the same position as the calf, the dam would quickly have removed her litter if fire or water threatened.

Horses are credited with sense, and we talk of someone wanting a little "horse sense". A thoroughbred mare and foal over three months old stood under a lot of sucker elms for shade all day during a heat wave and then grazed in the evening. One day, as the mare was still under the trees at the time she was usually grazing, an inspection was made, and the foal was found to be wedged between two young elm trees. The mare had pawed a hole in the ground, and made frantic efforts to get into a position for the foal to suck, but the trees were too thick. One person could easily lift or push the foal out, but like the calf in the dry ditch, the foal would have died without human aid.

The sheep on her back, with dozens of her companions sniffing her, but giving no help, also dies. The calf, the foal, and the sheep on her back could all have been saved by a timely push from the parent or another sheep, and some sad losses have been recorded for the want of it.

Whether a cow elephant would lift her young out of a pit or bog I do not know.

First published in the *West Sussex Gazette*, April 1965

Readers may recall the case of the young giraffe at London Zoo, some years ago, which fell and couldn't get up. Not only were the parents incapable of helping it, but even when it was hoisted onto its feet with a winch, it continued to weaken and ultimately died. It would have died in the wild, and even in captivity that expectation of death was too great to allow the animal to recover.

It is perhaps fitting that we should end this book, not only with one of Graburn's last articles, but also with an extract from his journal, which was the source for much of his published work. The following extract is one of the earliest, written in 1940, concerning the Field family of Burpham who were once famous as horse and cow "doctors". The family still live and farm in Burpham today. The following is reproduced as it was written down sixty-one years ago.

A friend told me how he employed G. Field for the first time, he had a cart colt covered with large warts, as big as cricket balls in some cases, a qualified vet had told him it was a big job and he would rather not do it, but to the farmer's dismay he arrived home from market and was told by one of his men that Field had been to see the colt, he then proceeded to the box and found the colt with every wort gone, and there in a box were the worts which nearly filled a gallon. When asked how he did it, he said, "we winds 'em out root and rind Sir,". This I can vouch for as I have seen him do the same thing, but not as many as in this case. G. Field left two sons, both are cow keepers but are not following the profession seriously, but do a little for neighbours. In the winter of 1937 G. Field was desperately ill, but when a little better told Dr. Pearson, he wanted to make a start again. To this the Doctor replied: "Field, I am a doctor." "So am I Sir," was the reply and when the doctor came again Field was gone to Nutbourne to see sick cattle. Field once met Professor Hobday the eminent vet at Mr. Butcher's, who the latter told me was impressed by his methods and that he enjoyed the consultation. [*George Field, grandson of the horse doctor, still runs Splash Farm today.*]

George Field died in April 1940 following the bitter winter of that year and was buried at Burpham; Graburn noted that he was the last of a long line of Fields who had been "horse and cow doctors". In common with so much of the custom and knowledge of a less material and "educated" age, these home-spun vets had no place in post-war England. Like a twentieth century Thomas Hardy, Lawrence Graburn chronicled the life and times of the English countryside as he had known it, recording people, places and events, that already, only thirty-six years after his death, have passed from living memory into history.

References

1   From taped interviews with Rosamund Hoy conducted during the summer of 2001
2   From taped interviews with Michael Hoy conducted during the summer of 2001
3   West Sussex Gazette, 6 November 1873
4   West Sussex Gazette, 3 June 1954
5   West Sussex Gazette, 3 June 1954
6   West Sussex Gazette,10 June 1954 (Further readers letters on the topic of Rough Music also appeared in the West Sussex Gazette on 24 June 1954).
7   John Cowper Powys, Autobiography, (John Lane, Bodley Head), London 1934, p.317
8   Evening Argus, 24 November 1967
9   Article in West Sussex Gazette, 2 November 1961, regarding the retirement of Mrs. Mariner.
10 West Sussex Gazette, October 1959
11 West Sussex Gazette, 29 August 1957
12 William Alberry, A Millennium of Facts in the History of Horsham and Sussex (Alberry), Horsham 1947, pp 295-296.
13 Interview with Nobby Kinnard of Patching, recorded 12 July 1999
14 John Cowper Powys, p.328
15 Referred to in Lawrie Graburn's journal, now in the possession of Mrs. Rosamund Hoy.
16 Sir Harry Johnston, The Story of My Life (Chatto & Windus), London 1923, pp 509-510.
17 As reported in Sussex Weekly Advertiser 23 January 1849
18 Nobby Kinnard, 12 July 1999
19 John Cowper Powys, pp 361-363
20 Tickner Edwardes, Neighbourhood (Methuen), London 191 1, pp 145-146
21 W H Hudson, Nature in Downland (J M Dent & Sons), London 1925 (first published by Longmans, Green & Co, 1900)
22 W H Hudson, p. 119
23 John Cowper Powys, pp 325-326
24 John Cowper Powys, p. 324
25 John Cowper Powys, pp. 318-319
26 Tickner Edwardes, A Downland Year (Methuen), London 1939, pp 237-238
27 Tickner Edwardes, A Country Calendar (John Lane the Bodley Head Ltd.), London 1928, pp 275-276
28 Reported in the Worthing Gazette, 27 May 1914.
29 Mentioned in letter published in the West Sussex Gazette, 30 May 1957, written by Francis Foster of West Chiltington.
30 West Sussex Gazette, 10 January 1957.
31 Sussex Notes & Queries, Vol. 4, 1933, pp 186-187.
32 Rev. W D Parish, A Dictionary of the Sussex Dialect and Collection of Provincialisms in the County of Sussex (Farncombe & Co.), London 1875.
33 Mrs. Charlotte Latham, Some West Sussex Superstitions Lingering in 1868 (Folklore Society), London 1878, pp 10-11.

INDEX

(Numbers in italic refer to illustrations)